ROB DRAPER, ACS

A HAIR IN THE GATE

A VETERAN DP'S JOURNEY
THROUGH THE ART AND THE
MAYHEM OF FILMMAKING

ROB DRAPER, ACS

ROB DRAPER, ACS

PUBLISHED BY: REVOLUTION DIGITAL

No part of this publication may be copied, reproduced in any format, by any means, electronic or otherwise, without prior consent from the copyright owner and publisher of this book.

Copyright © 2024 Rob Draper, ACS
All rights reserved.

FOREWORD

In the world of filmmaking, the phrase "a hair in the gate" strikes a unique kind of panic on set, an uninvited guest capable of halting an entire production. Back in the days of film cameras, the "gate" referred to the small opening in front of the camera's film plane. Here, light would pass through the lens, hitting the film stock to expose each frame. In theory, it should be a clear path—just the camera's lens and the film stock meeting in an intricate dance of light and movement. But sometimes, a small obstruction would make its way into the scene, catching itself in the gate—a rogue hair, dust particle, or even a tiny fiber.

If you've ever watched a film and noticed a strange, blurry line that seems to persist scene after scene, you've glimpsed the effects of a hair in the gate. That tiny interference, if not caught by the assistant cameraman during filming, would appear on every frame, or until the magazine was changed, marring the image and rendering the footage unusable at worst or leaving the scene with a flickering dancing hair at the top of the frame. Following what the director considered to be the "print" take the AD would call "check the gate". Then by either pulling the lens, looking down the barrel of the lens or sometimes opening the camera and gently lifting the film off the registration pins to physically see the gate, the 1st AC would check. This last method was not preferred however because moving the film could potentially remove any debris or a hair and the offending object would be missed….until the film was seen in dailies and there it would be, dancing around generally at the top of the frame. Either way the assistant would check and he or she could see if there was anything caught on the edge of the gate….if there was then "Hair in the Gate" was announced, if not "gate's clean" and on we would go.

When an assistant cameraman (AC) announced "Hair in the Gate", the brakes would go on the entire production. It was as if a locomotive suddenly hit the brakes and wheels were grinding, sparks flying. Everyone, from the director to the actors and crew, would hold their breath while the camera crew opened up the camera, inspected the gate, and cleaned out any debris, ensuring a clear path for the next take.

This simple phrase became a reminder of the high stakes and precision required on set, even in the smallest details. If caught early, a hair in the gate could be removed with minimal disruption. But if discovered too late—after an entire scene was filmed—it meant a disturbing distraction in the finished frame or possibly a reshoot if it was particularly bad. For this reason AC's were meticulous about keeping the camera, the magazines and the environment around the camera, very clean.

In the pages of this book, *A Hair in the Gate*, you'll find stories of chaos, misadventures, and the unexpected moments that bring a film set to life. Much like the literal hair in the gate, these stories capture the beauty, the humor, and, occasionally, the pandemonium that happens just outside the frame.

I have written this as a series of short stories in no particular order so feel free to skip around and digest them as the mood takes…thank you for coming along on my journey.

Rob Draper, ACS
Director of Photography

To my wife of 51 years, Sue and Sons Ben and Paul for keeping on my back for 30 years to write this.

ROB DRAPER, ACS

TABLE OF CONTENTS

FOREWORD 7
ASTONISHED 15
TIGER WARSAW 19
HALLOWEEN 5 35
AMAZING GRACE 43
CLOSE ENCOUNTERS OF THE SPIELBERG KIND 49
STEAMY DAYS IN THE TROPICS 53
100 SHOTS 69
TARPS, TORNADOS AND TOPEKA 75
PIRATES, PARROTS AND GOLD DUBLOONS 83
THE PITTSBURGH HEIST 89
BOOT PRINTS IN THE DIRT 93
SPRINGTIME IN MALLORCA 97
SELF PRESERVATION 103
A BRIDGE TOO FAR 111
WINTER IN NEWARK 113
WISH YOU WERE HERE 123
BABY ON THE BOSPHORUS 127
COULD YOU PASS THE ROMANÉE CONTI? 137
SHORT ENDS 141
ABOUT THE AUTHOR 167

ASTONISHED

WELCOME TO NYC

My first feature film gig came hot on the heels of shooting Season 1 of *Tales From the Darkside*. It wasn't exactly a dream project—non-union, ultra-low budget, shooting in Manhattan in the dead of winter. But I was hungry for the experience, willing to take whatever came my way, and I had a vision for how I could give the story a strong visual style. Plus, a feature was a feature, and I wasn't in a position to turn it down.

I pulled most of my crew from *Darkside*, guys I trusted to get the job done under rough conditions. We had a four-week shoot ahead of us, and we all knew it was going to be a grind. The Director, bless his heart, was an actor with absolutely zero experience behind the camera. The producer? He was the son of a dentist, with no producing experience to speak of either. His dad had handed him $250,000, basically to go play movie maker. But hey, it was enough to get the cameras rolling, and I was ready to make the most of it.

From the get-go, the production was every bit the struggle you'd expect.

There was no money, no luxuries, a skeleton crew, and the kind of bitter cold that only New York City in the middle of winter can serve up. We scraped by on enthusiasm, ingenuity, and a shared love of filmmaking—until everything came crashing down.

It was a Saturday before our last week of shooting, and I was at home in New Jersey, trying to thaw out from the freezing week we'd just wrapped. My phone rang. I picked up, and on the other end, the producer's voice came through. "Hey, Rob, how's it going?"

"Oh, pretty good," I replied. "What's up?"

"You're fired."

I laughed, waiting for the punchline. But there was no punchline or laugh back, just a pause. He wasn't joking.

"We're going in a different direction," I replied, "a different direction what the hell does that mean" , he continued, his tone almost businesslike, like he'd practiced it in the mirror.

One week away from wrapping, and they'd decided I had too much control over how the film was being shot. Which, honestly, was probably true—I was the only one who actually knew how to shoot a film.

They wanted someone with experience but apparently I had too much experience for them, but I was there, grinding out each shot, making sure they'd have something that would actually cut together in the editing room. I wasn't dealing with the actors; I was just trying to make sure they had what they needed to cut a movie together.

So that was it. The first time I'd ever been fired, and for what? Doing my job too well? I called up my crew, who had been with me through the worst of it, and told them what happened. Without hesitation, they all quit too. Solidarity in the face of chaos. We'd worked together through freezing nights and endless takes, and they weren't about to see it through without me.

The whole thing was surreal. I spent that Saturday shaking my head, wondering how in the world it had all gone sideways. But then, a few weeks later, I learned the real reason behind my firing. The producer had a friend—someone who fancied himself a cinematographer. He figured this was the perfect chance to give his buddy a shot and I guess ride on the coattails of what had already been shot. So he booted me, and brought his friend in for that final week of shooting.

Of course, there was a catch: the new guy was stuck trying to match the footage I'd shot for the first three weeks. It was like giving a guy the last piece of a puzzle without showing him the box.

Welcome to the film industry. It wasn't the last time I'd encounter this brand of Hollywood madness, but it sure was a hell of a way to get my start.

The film was later named "Astonished" which couldn't have been more appropriate.

TIGER WARSAW

THE INTERVIEW
SUNSET ON 42ⁿᵈ STREET

When I got the call for an interview, I could hardly contain my excitement. The project was *Tiger Warsaw*, starring the up-and-coming Patrick Swayze, alongside Piper Laurie, Lee Richardson, and Bobby DiCicco. It was a solid cast, a real film—an opportunity I couldn't ignore. As I made my way down 42nd Street, weaving through the familiar chaos around the Port Authority, the anticipation only grew.

The sun was low in the sky, casting the kind of golden light that turns New York City into a stage, with 42nd Street as its glowing centerline, like a spotlight cutting through the concrete canyons. It disappeared behind the silhouette of New Jersey, leaving the city wrapped in a warm, nostalgic glow.

I reached the towering green marble facade of the McGraw-Hill building, feeling that thrill you get when the stakes are high and you're on the edge of something new. *Penthouse Suite,* I thought, growing more impressed by the second. This was clearly no small-time operation.

A friendly young woman met me in the lobby and offered coffee before leading me up in a sleek elevator, higher and higher until the city below seemed like a distant memory. As the elevator doors slid open, I was ushered into a stunning office—floor-to-ceiling windows framing Manhattan like a living, breathing postcard. The Hudson River shimmered in the last rays of the sun, the city bathed in twilight. It was breathtaking, and I could feel my pulse quicken with the potential of what lay ahead.

Then, The Director made his entrance. He was an Indian gentleman, dressed head to toe in white—white suit, white shoes, a crisply tied cravat, and a white Panama hat perched on his head. He stepped out from behind a grand desk that seemed to command the room, extended his hand, and greeted me with a warm, confident smile. As I shook his hand, he asked me a question that caught me off guard.

"So, who do I look like?" he asked, as if it was the most natural thing in the world.

I blinked, momentarily thrown off balance. My mind raced—*What kind of question is that?* It wasn't exactly your typical interview opener. I fumbled for a reply, but before I could piece together an answer, he filled in the silence himself.

"Don't I remind you of David Lean?" he said, with a touch of self-assurance that filled the room. He straightened his cravat as if to emphasize the point. And right then, something in my gut twisted—a warning, maybe, that this might not be what I had envisioned. I should have bolted, made a polite excuse, and left.

But the allure of a big film, the penthouse office, and that sunset view over Manhattan held me in place. I stayed, drawn into the whirlpool of what would become one of the most memorable—and unpredictable—experiences of my career.

TELL ME YOUR VISION

The Director offered me a seat across from him at an enormous, polished table that gleamed in the last light of the day. He rocked back in his chair, leaned all the way back until it creaked under the strain, then swung his feet up onto the desk, crossing them casually as he stared me down. His expression was somewhere between smug and inquisitive.

"Describe your vision of the film," he said, as if it was a challenge.

Now, I always prep extensively for these things—especially an interview for a feature like *Tiger Warsaw*.

I'd dissected the script, gone through every detail, and jotted down pages of notes. So, I launched into my overview, talking about the broad strokes of the film's tone and visual style. But I hadn't gotten more than a few sentences out before he cut me off, waving a hand in the air.

"No," he said, sitting up straighter, his tone suddenly sharp, "Describe *every* scene to me." I blinked. "What, every scene?" My brain scrambled to keep up. We would be here for hours, maybe all night. "Do you mean literally every scene?"

He leaned back again, folding his arms behind his head, and smirked. "Yes, are you in a hurry?"

It wasn't really a question. He was testing me, and I wasn't about to back down. So, I took a deep breath and began. The sun had dipped below the skyline, leaving Manhattan draped in that brief, magical hour where the sky turns cotton-candy pink and the city's lights start to twinkle awake. The World Trade Center stood silhouetted against the dusky sky as I launched into scene after scene, describing every shot, every camera movement, every shift in light and shadow.

Time stretched on, and I kept talking, painting each frame with words. At some point, The Director leaned forward and asked, almost playfully, "Do you need an intermission?"

I shook my head and kept going. The city outside dimmed, and the window turned from a canvas of fiery colors to a reflection of the room, capturing my relentless recital as the night wrapped around us. Below, Manhattan became a sparkling carpet of lights, and I was barely aware of it—I was lost in the rhythm of my own words, committed to getting through this unorthodox interrogation.

Finally, after nearly three hours, I reached the end. "Fade out," I said, my voice hoarse from talking. I took a deep breath, letting the silence fill the room. For a moment, all I heard was the hum of the city far below us. The Director stood up slowly, the chair groaning beneath him as he unfolded himself from it. He walked over, extended his hand, and looked me straight in the eye. "That is exactly how I see the film," he said, his voice as smooth as a cool summer breeze slipping through an open window.

That should have been my second warning right there—when a director, without a single adjustment or critique, tells you that a three-hour monologue about his own movie matches his vision perfectly. But before I could fully process the unease gnawing at my gut, he followed up with the words that sealed the deal: "You will be my cinematographer."

And that's how I found myself strapped into one of the strangest and most unpredictable rides of my career.

ON PATRICK SWAYZE.

Before delving into Tiger Warsaw I have to preface what follows by saying Patrick was one of the nicest, most sincere and likeable people I have ever met. He was an absolute joy to work with and we got on great together with both of us, much of the time, feeling the same pressures. We shared a lot of laughs and what was great is Patrick had a very Aussie sense of humor which made our time together in the trenches bearable.

CALLING 911

It was a typical day on set, filming in a small, slightly rundown motel on the edge of town. The crew was set up for a particularly intense scene with Patrick Swayze, where he played a character who had reached the end of his rope. The atmosphere was heavy—perfect for the mood of the scene. Patrick's character was supposed to make a desperate phone call, the kind where you lay your soul bare, revealing to the stranger on the other end that you've got a handful of pills and no intention of seeing tomorrow.

As we rolled cameras, Patrick picked up the phone, dialed the number written in the script, and launched into his monologue, pouring out a heartfelt, sorrowful confession about his plans to end it all. The scene was raw, authentic—so much so that I remember thinking, "Wow, he's really in it today."

But then, something strange happened. Instead of the quiet, scripted silence of an imaginary phone call, there was a voice on the other end. Patrick had accidentally dialed a real number, and the person on the other end was very much alive—and very confused.

Staying in character, Patrick kept going, improvising around the bewildered responses of the stranger. He mentioned the name of the motel we were filming in, dropped some heartfelt words about how he couldn't go on, and then hung up with a shaky sigh, adding an unexpected layer of realism to the scene. When we called "cut," he put the phone down, turned to us with wide eyes, and said, "I think I might've just scared the hell out of some poor guy."

We all had a laugh, thinking it would end there—just another weird behind-the-scenes story to tell. But about five minutes later, the sound of sirens pierced the air, and a couple of squad cars pulled up to the front of the motel, lights flashing. Turns out, the stranger on the phone had believed every word Patrick said. He'd called the police, genuinely worried that someone was about to take his own life at our exact location.

The officers burst in, ready for an emergency, only to find us all standing around, film equipment everywhere, and Patrick Swayze sheepishly waving at them in a half-apology, half-greeting.

There was an awkward pause as the situation sank in, and we tried to explain that it was all just part of a movie. The officers exchanged a look, and then, maybe recognizing Patrick from one of his many iconic roles, they finally cracked a smile.

We all ended up sharing a laugh over the bizarre turn of events, but it definitely made for a story none of us would ever forget. It's not every day that an actor's performance is so convincing, it warrants an emergency response!

LITTLE BLACK CORVETTE

Another hilarious story from the set of *Tiger Warsaw* involved a scene with Patrick's character in that classic black Chevy Corvette Stingray. The shot was simple enough on paper: Patrick was supposed to drive to an intersection, see a sign, make a right turn, and leave town. Off to the left of that sign, in a dusty, desolate parking lot, was the entire crew—well, sort of.

The Director, in his usual uniform of a pristine white suit, white Panama hat, and flowing pink silk scarf, sat alone in a director's chair.

He had his legs crossed, looking every bit the picture of a Hollywood auteur. By that stage of the production, however, the crew had taken to keeping their distance, so he sat there isolated, a figure of authority… and irritation.

I was in the back of the Corvette with the camera, pulling double duty as both the DP and the camera operator on this film. The Director, who'd been driving Patrick up the wall for days, was barking out instructions over a walkie-talkie, his voice crackling with that ever-present insistence.

As Patrick sat behind the wheel, revving the engine and waiting for the cue to go, he leaned toward me with a mischievous grin and said, "I'm going to drive straight at that bastard when we take off from the intersection."

I couldn't help but laugh and suggested that maybe that wasn't the best idea. But Patrick just kept smiling, a twinkle in his eye, and said, "If you kill a director, is it murder or manslaughter? Or do they just say, 'Oh, that was understandable'?"

We shared a good laugh, and then the assistant director called, "Action!" Patrick gunned the engine and headed for the intersection, turning to look in the rearview mirror at me. With a wink, he said, "Watch this."

Instead of turning right as scripted, he cranked the wheel to the left and aimed the car directly at The Director, who was still sitting calmly in his chair, legs crossed. At first, The Director just sat there, thinking it was part of the act. But as the Corvette got closer, the reality of the situation started to sink in. His serene expression turned to wide-eyed panic as he leapt out of the chair, scrambling for cover.

Patrick and I were in stitches, laughing so hard that I almost missed the shot entirely. It was one of those moments you couldn't plan for—another fun day on set with Patrick's wicked sense of humor keeping everyone on their toes.

THE TAMING OF THE......

One of the most surreal days on the set of *Tiger Warsaw* started with a 6 a.m. call time. Everyone arrived early, bleary-eyed but ready to get set up for the first shot of the day. The Director, ever the picture of dramatic flair in his David Lean-esque outfit—white suit, pink silk scarf fluttering in the morning breeze—called for a rehearsal before filming.

The scene was set in a small, ground-floor building with three apartments, so the crew gathered outside while The Director worked through the scene with the two actors inside—one male, one female. We expected a quick run-through, but as time dragged on, the rehearsal stretched past the one-hour mark, then longer. The male actor eventually left, leaving The Director alone with the actress inside the apartment.

By this point, all of us outside could hear snippets of their conversation about the scene. But things quickly took a turn when The Director's tone shifted from professional to aggressive.

He started screaming, yelling, and hurling abuse at the actress, and it went on and on, echoing through the thin walls.

We exchanged awkward glances outside, caught somewhere between disbelief and concern. Eventually, the actress had enough, storming out of the apartment, her footsteps ringing out in the otherwise quiet morning.

A few minutes later, The Director reemerged, standing on the porch like a general surveying the battlefield.

He planted his hands on his hips, tilted his chin skyward, and with his pink scarf billowing behind him in the breeze, declared triumphantly, "I know how to handle women!" And with that, he walked off, leaving the crew and the assistant director behind with jaws dropped.

The AD turned to us and, with a knowing sigh, said, "This is going to be a while." By now, we were two hours into our day, and we hadn't even rolled a single frame. Stories started circulating through the crew—rumors that the actress had called her lawyers, manager, and agent, and might be leaving the film altogether.

The day dragged on, with The Director periodically reappearing to assure us that everything was under control, insisting that they were just "working out some minor issues."

Next thing we knew, it was lunchtime, and still not a single shot had been filmed. The crew gathered on the lawn outside the apartments, eating our sandwiches while keeping an eye on the ongoing drama.

By the time word came down that everyone was "ready" to start shooting, it was nearly 6 p.m. That meant a full 12 hours had gone by, and still, not a single camera had rolled. At that point, the crew collectively decided that enough was enough. We stood up, announced that it was time to call it a day, and headed home.

The next day, we all returned to the set, hoping for a more productive start.

The actors showed up, and we finally prepared to roll on the first shot.

This time, the scene was being directed by the 1st AD. Just as we were about to start, The Director appeared again, his trademark scarf trailing behind him. He wasn't allowed on set when the actress was present anymore, but as producer, he was still allowed to be "in the vicinity."

So, with a flair only he could muster, he walked straight onto the set, opened a closet door, and stepped inside. "Close the door behind me," he instructed one of the crew members.

The door shut with a creak, and all was silent for a moment. We got ready to roll, but then, muffled through the closet door, came a familiar voice: "Action!"

It was one of those moments you couldn't make up—a director, banned from set, calling the shots from inside a closet while we tried to keep straight faces. It was just another day in the bizarre world of *Tiger Warsaw*.

PRIVATE SCREENING AT THE ZEIGFIELD THEATER.

The Ziegfeld wasn't just any cinema; it was one of the most prestigious theaters in New York City, a place where film legends had their premieres. It had plush red seats, an enormous screen that seemed to stretch to the edges of your vision, and the finest THX sound system in the city. When you sat in that theater, you felt like you were in the presence of movie royalty. And today, it was set to host the opening day of *Tiger Warsaw*, a film I'd poured my heart into.

This was the first movie released by Sony after their acquisition of Columbia Pictures.

I was excited to see the results myself, so I decided to go to the Ziegfeld on the first day. I pictured a line of eager moviegoers snaking down the block, waiting to see this story I had worked so hard to bring to life.

But when I arrived at the theater, the sidewalk out front was deserted. Not a soul in sight. I shrugged it off, thinking maybe I was just a little early. No big deal. I went up to the box office, bought my ticket, and stepped inside.

As I entered the auditorium, I looked around and saw row upon row of empty seats, stretching out in every direction. I figured maybe the crowd would show up closer to start time, so I picked a seat somewhere in the middle and waited.

Time passed. The theater stayed silent. Finally, I heard footsteps coming down the aisle, echoing in the vast, empty space. "Here we go," I thought, expecting the first trickle of the audience. But instead, it was just one person—a young man, the projectionist. He looked at me with a hint of awkwardness in his expression and said, "Hey, so… do you want me to run the movie? Nobody's here."

I was too embarrassed to tell him that I'd shot the film myself, that I was sitting there waiting to see my work on that magnificent screen. Instead, I forced a smile and said, "Yeah, I've heard it's a really good movie. I'd still love to see it."

"No problem," he replied, and headed back up to the projection booth.

So there I sat, alone in one of the most iconic theaters in New York, watching *Tiger Warsaw* unfold on that enormous screen.

The sound echoed beautifully in the space, the visuals looked stunning—everything I'd hoped it would be. But it was all playing to an audience of one. When the credits rolled, I shuffled out to the lobby, where the projectionist stood waiting, clearly unsure of how to wrap up this strange encounter. "Thanks for running the movie," I mumbled, still too embarrassed to explain my connection to it.

He nodded politely, and I stepped outside, blinking in the harsh light of the New York afternoon. I decided to take a walk, try to clear my head. As I rounded the corner, I found myself in front of another nearby theater. And this one was different—there was a long line stretching down the block, buzzing with excitement, people chatting eagerly as they waited to get in.

The ever so clever studio executives had come up with a really tricky strategy. They had caught wind that Patrick Swayze had another movie coming out, and they decided to delay *Tiger Warsaw*'s release, hoping that it would ride the momentum of his newfound popularity. The thinking was, if people loved seeing Swayze on screen once, they'd come back for more.

Patrick's "other" film…..*Dirty Dancing*

HALLOWEEN 5

HAMSTRINGS AND WARM BEER

We were nearing the end of the *Halloween 5* shoot, working on a remote farm about 40 miles outside of Salt Lake City. It was one of those punishing night shoots—cold, endless, with that unsettling quiet that made it feel like Michael Myers might be lurking just beyond the lights. The night dragged on, and at one point, our Best Boy Electric pulled his hamstring. He spent most of the night sidelined, wincing in pain while the rest of us ground through the last few shots.

As the sky finally began to lighten, washing the Wasatch Mountains in a soft lavender glow, the AD called wrap. Relief swept through the set like a warm breeze, and everyone started packing up, eager to head back to the hotel for a few precious hours of sleep.

The Best Boy Electric, despite his injury, somehow ended up behind the wheel of our crew van. It was non-union, so everyone pitched in where needed, and that meant he got the driver's seat. I jumped into the van with The Director Dominique, the Gaffer, the Key Grip, the Best Boy Grip, and my 1st AC. It was a tight squeeze, but at that point, we'd have crammed ourselves into a clown car if it meant getting off that farm.

The Gaffer, always prepared, had stashed a few beers, and as we hit the highway, he started passing them around. Tired as we were, the mood in the van lifted as we popped the caps and leaned back into our seats, sharing stories from the night's shoot. We roared down the Utah Interstate, headlights cutting through the dawn, casting a warm glow on the road ahead.

The Best Boy Electric, who had been nursing that sore leg all night, seemed to find his stride behind the wheel. Soon, we realized he was pushing the van well over 100 miles per hour, and we were flying down the highway. The cold, early morning air rushed in through the cracked windows as we laughed, beer in hand, swapping tales of on-set disasters and near-misses.

It was one of those moments of camaraderie—exhausted but giddy, the kind of scene where everything feels just a little bit surreal. The Wasatch mountains were silhouetted against a sky turning from inky blue to pink, and the whole scene seemed to glow with the promise of morning.

But then, another glow joined the scene—a red and blue flash that filled the van like a strobe light. We all turned to see a police cruiser hot on our tail, its lights flashing across the interior, turning our impromptu party into something out of a buddy comedy gone wrong.

The van went quiet as we realized what was happening, and then, in perfect timing, someone muttered, "Well, this should be interesting." A beat of silence hung in the air before we all cracked up, unable to hold back the laughter even as the sirens wailed behind us.

It turned out, we didn't just have one cop car tailing us—it was three, and as I glanced out the rear window, the scene unfolding behind us looked like something straight out of *The Dukes of Hazzard*. Red and blue lights flashed through the darkness, illuminating the empty Utah highway like a chaotic disco. It only made the situation funnier, and the whole van erupted in laughter, unable to contain ourselves as the Best Boy Electric eased the van to a stop.

As the vehicles came to a halt, we scrambled to hide our beers—stuffing bottles under seats, jackets, anywhere we could think of. One of the bottles tipped over, and suddenly the van reeked like a mobile bar. Realizing the jig was up, we all decided to down whatever beer we had left as quickly as possible, hoping to hide the evidence.

The first officer approached the driver's side, his expression stony, clearly not amused. He shone his flashlight into the van, catching sight of the Best Boy Electric at the wheel. "What the hell do you think you're doing?" he barked.

The Best Boy gave what he probably thought was an innocent enough answer: "I was just driving back to the hotel."

"At 100 miles per hour?" the officer shot back.

And then the Best Boy gave the worst possible reply. "I needed to go to the bathroom."

We couldn't help ourselves—everyone in the van burst out laughing, howling at the absurdity of it all. The officer's face went red with frustration, and he growled, "So you lot think this is a joke? Driver, get out of the vehicle."

The Best Boy tried to play up his injury, clutching his leg dramatically. "I can't get out, officer. I've got a sore leg."

The cop wasn't having any of it. "If you don't get out right now, I'll drag you out myself."

Reluctantly, the Best Boy hobbled out of the van and shuffled to the back, where the officers promptly put him through a field sobriety test. It was not going well—he could barely stand, let alone walk in a straight line, and the flashing lights of the police cars made it look like a scene from a B-movie.

Meanwhile, in the van, Dominique—The Director—suddenly announced, "Oh, I have to take a piss."

We all turned to him and hissed, "You can't! They're right there!"

But he wasn't to be deterred. "I can't wait. Pass me a bottle," he demanded, as if it were the most reasonable request in the world.

Just as Dominique was finishing up his business in the bottle, another officer approached the van. "Okay, everyone out of the van and line up between the vehicles," he ordered.

So there we were, lined up like a bunch of delinquent school kids, the morning light creeping over the horizon, while one of the officers started to give us a stern lecture. "I guess you're the film people shooting that movie," he grumbled. "We can tell because none of you drive under 100 miles per hour.

Admittedly, you weren't going as fast as the stunt guys we pulled over two days ago, but you were still 50 miles over the speed limit. Now, is anyone doing drugs?"

We all shook our heads vigorously. "No, officer."

"Anyone been drinking?" he pressed.

Again, the chorus of, "No, officer."

He wasn't buying it. "Well, we're going to search the van. Is there anything we should know about?"

At that moment, Dominique decided it was time to make his presence known. He stepped forward and, in his thick French accent, declared, "My name is Dominique, and I am a citizen of France."

The officer shot him a flat look. "Lucky you. Now get back in line."

As two officers headed back to the van to start searching, the Key Grip leaned over to me and whispered, "Oh shit, this is not good… I have a joint in my bag."

We all tensed up, hoping that little detail wouldn't come back to bite us. Meanwhile, one of the officers called back from the van, holding up a half-empty bottle. "So you *have* been drinking alcohol? You could've at least chilled it!" He poured it out dramatically onto the asphalt, completely unaware of the actual contents. We had to stifle our laughter, biting our lips to keep from cracking up again.

The search continued as the officers collected the bottles, assembling them like evidence in a prohibition bust. Then, searching through a backpack they found the joint. One officer held it up between two fingers and asked, "Whose is this?"

The Key Grip, thinking fast, put on his best innocent face. "It's my girlfriend's! She lives in New York City—she must've left it in my bag."

After another stern lecture, the officers eventually decided to cut us some slack. "We are tired of you film people," one of them barked, "but we've been told to go easy on you because apparently Utah needs films to shoot here. But you tell your producers this: if we pull over another vehicle associated with that movie for *any* reason, everyone inside will be arrested, and the movie will be shut down. Now get back in the van, have someone who isn't the cripple drive, stay at or under the speed limit, and we will escort you back to the hotel. We don't want to see any of your ugly faces ever again."

And just like that, they piled us back into the van, gave us a police escort down the highway back to the hotel. We arrived just after the stunt guys who were getting out of their van, they saw the cops, the same cops who had pulled them over a few days earlier. They smiled and waved….the cops weren't impressed.

AMAZING GRACE

THANKSGIVING IN COEUR D'ALENE WITH BURT REYNOLDS

I'd worked with Patty Duke on several films by then, and we got along famously. She was a joy to be around—smart, funny, and as sharp as they come. So, when she approached me to shoot a new TV series she'd be both producing and starring in, I wasn't surprised. But, to be honest, I wasn't all that eager to commit. We were filming a movie at the time, and during takes, she would drop hints about it. Between scenes, she'd bring it up, and once, she even got down on her knees in front of the camera, mock-begging me to join the series.

By the end of the shoot, she'd worn me down, and I finally agreed. Coeur d'Alene sounded like a lovely spot to spend a few months, and I figured it wouldn't be so bad working on a project with someone I already had great chemistry with.

I headed up with my crew, prepped for the series, and started shooting. My wife, Sue, and our kids, Ben and Paul, came along as well, making it a bit of a working family adventure.

November rolled around, and Patty, always thoughtful, arranged a special birthday dinner for

Sue on the 16th at a beautiful mountain restaurant overlooking the lake. She even offered to babysit Ben and Paul for the evening. It was an offer too good to pass up. Sue and I had an unforgettable night—gorgeous views, fantastic food, and the rare luxury of a night out, just the two of us, thanks to Patty.

Another time, Patty's husband planned a helicopter trip to Spokane, taking their kids to a concert, and he invited Ben and Paul to join them. Our boys were over the moon—flying in a chopper to a concert, and with Patty Duke's family, no less! It was the highlight of their stay, and we couldn't have asked for a warmer welcome from the Duke family.

It was a special time in Coeur d'Alene, thanks to Patty's warmth, generosity, and unshakeable spirit. I couldn't have imagined a more memorable way to work on that series or a better experience for our family.

Of course, good times in the film industry never seem to last. We were filming a six-episode pilot series in Coeur d'Alene with Patty Duke, each episode shot over five days.

Patty, both the star and producer, had convinced me to sign on, and it was shaping up to be an interesting project.

Every week we brought in a special guest star to add some excitement, and by the time we hit Episode 4, we'd built up a good rhythm. The guest star for this episode was none other than Burt Reynolds, playing the role of a flamboyant televangelist. Burt arrived on set, larger than life, his personality electric, and perfectly suited for the role.

Burt was a true professional—a warm, funny, respectful guy who had the whole crew captivated from the start. By day three, everyone was singing his praises, and I got on with him famously. But that was about the time Patty started acting a bit off. She seemed tense and a little on edge, though none of us could put a finger on why. I chalked it up to the pressures of producing and starring simultaneously, figuring she was just tired.

On Friday morning, the last day of the episode, I was having breakfast when the Key Grip, who'd worked with me for seven years by then, mentioned that he'd seen another film crew out in town the previous night, having dinner at one of the local restaurants. Coeur d'Alene was small; it seemed odd that another crew would be here. We assumed they were probably just scouting the area.

Lunchtime came, and Patty finished her scenes for the day.

We only had a few more shots to grab with Burt and his "congregation" in the church.

As I was enjoying lunch, the UPM sent word that he wanted to see me in his office. I reluctantly pulled myself away from swapping tall tales with Burt, chuckling over the adventures of our respective careers.

When I arrived, the UPM looked grave. He closed the door, sighed, and said, "Rob, I hate to tell you this, but Patty has fired you. She wants you to finish the day and then leave."

I was floored. "You're joking, right?"

"No, I'm afraid not," he replied. "She says you're welcome to take your time leaving Coeur d'Alene, but she doesn't want you within 20 miles of the set come Monday, and if you're closer, she won't work."

My jaw dropped. "This has to be a joke."

But it wasn't. The UPM explained that the crew my Key Grip had seen in town was actually my replacement crew. Patty had fired not just me but the entire team I'd brought up with me. Come Monday, they would have a new crew on set.

Since I had all my 35mm gear on the show—two full Arri 535 packages—I was told I'd have to pack everything up.

The next day, they drove the camera truck to a warehouse outside town where I could pack up my gear without breaching the 20-mile radius. I was still at the production office when they informed me of all this, and after getting directions to the warehouse, I headed out to my car, still dazed by what had happened.

Just as I reached the car, I heard a faint whisper, "Psst! Rob! Over here…" I turned and, peering through the bushes, spotted Dan Lauria, who played the male lead and had become a close friend, alongside Joe Spano, crouching like a couple of fugitives.

They waved me over, and Dan whispered, "Hey, Rob, we just wanted to say we're so sorry about all this. We just heard the full story, and believe us, we're as confused as you are. We're hiding out here because if Patty sees us talking to you, we're afraid she might fire us, too. She's gone a little bonkers."

I asked if they had any idea why she'd decided to fire me, but they shook their heads. They'd heard nothing that made any sense. We shared a brief, conspiratorial chat, and then they snuck back through the bushes like a couple of school kids sneaking out after curfew.

Curious, I went back to the UPM, a good guy who seemed just as bewildered as I was.

When I asked him if he had any idea what was going on, he hesitated before finally explaining, "Patty felt that when Burt turned up, you and the crew seemed to like him more than her, so she decided to fire you for 'not being loyal.'"

I couldn't help but laugh at the absurdity of it. This was the same Patty Duke who'd practically begged me to join the show, who'd thrown a birthday dinner for my wife, Sue, who had hosted us at her home and arranged helicopter rides for my kids. And now, because Burt's charm had captivated the set, she had declared us disloyal. Who says the film industry isn't a bizarre place to work?

And there's a postscript to this story. About eight years later, I got a call from a young lady asking if I was available to shoot a TV movie. I told her I was interested, and asked what the project was about.

"Well," she said, "I can send over the script. Patty Duke is starring in it and producing. She'd really love for you to be the DP—she absolutely loves your work."

It probably goes without saying what I told her.

CLOSE ENCOUNTERS OF THE SPIELBERG KIND

I found myself in Topeka, Kansas, for the fifth time, shooting another production for Len Hill. This time, it was a two-part miniseries called *A Matter of Justice*, directed by my longtime friend Michael Switzer. This wasn't our first rodeo together; we'd collaborated on six or seven projects by then, so there was an easy rhythm between us. We had an impressive cast on board too—Martin Sheen, Patty Duke, Jason London, Charles S. Dutton, and Alexandra Powers. The performances were stellar, and by the time we wrapped, we felt like we'd captured something special.

A few weeks later, I was called in for the color grade, and it was exciting to see everything come together. Michael would pop in occasionally to check the progress, but once the grade was complete, I called him to say, "The show looks fantastic and plays really well—looks like a winner all around."

Not long after the series aired, I got a call from Michael. He sounded a little dazed. "You won't believe this," he said. "Steven Spielberg called my agent. He wants to talk to me about the show."

"Are you serious?"

"Dead serious. He absolutely loved it. I have a meeting with him next week."

The news was huge, and I joked that he shouldn't forget me when he became famous. The following week, I was on pins and needles waiting to hear how the meeting went. Eventually, the call came through. Michael sounded both excited and bewildered.

"Spielberg loved the show," he said. "He went through the entire series in such detail that I was astounded. He remembered it all so clearly, just from one viewing."

"That's incredible," I said.

Michael continued, "And he specifically commented on how beautifully crafted it was— 'you and your DP crafted a really beautiful show,' he told me. He even said he wanted to work with us both on a project. He'd be in touch."

It was a blend of high excitement and a hint of letdown. Spielberg had seen our work, appreciated it, and expressed a desire to collaborate. It was a huge compliment, even if there was no immediate project attached.

Weeks turned into months, and life went on.

Then, out of the blue, Michael called me with an update. Spielberg had reached out again and wanted a meeting—nothing specific, just a chance to chat. The anticipation was back in full swing, and we all felt that this could be the big break.

The day of the meeting arrived, and I waited eagerly for Michael's call afterward to hear how it went. Eventually, the phone rang.

"So?" I asked.

"Well, we sat and talked movies for about 90 minutes. He knew my work in detail. It was surreal."

"Did he mention a specific movie?"

Michael paused, a sigh in his voice. "No, not a word about a project, which was a bummer."

"What *did* you talk about, then?" I asked.

"Oh, a bit of everything. But the funny part was when he asked me how I liked working with kids and animals."

Curious, I asked, "What did you tell him?"

"I told him the truth. I don't like working with kids, and I hate working with animals

There was a beat of stunned silence on my end. "Wait, you actually told *Steven Spielberg* that?"

"Yeah… and right after I said it, I thought maybe that wasn't the best answer," he admitted sheepishly.

And that was that. Spielberg never called again, and the dream project that seemed so close drifted out of reach. But at least we knew he'd seen our work and loved it—and we learned an unspoken rule of the film industry: if Spielberg ever asks if you like working with kids and animals, the answer is a resounding, "Absolutely!"

STEAMY DAYS IN THE TROPICS

In the early 80s, I spent about six weeks in the Philippines shooting beer and cigarette commercials. It was an unforgettable experience, working with an enthusiastic, hardworking local crew and a Chinese agency. I always had plenty of grips, 20-30 would arrive every morning and stand, at ease, forming a line along the studio wall and peeling off one by one as needed. They were paid as and if they worked, I think around $1/day. Naning was experienced, a Filipino named Naning.

LONG PANTS AND HAIRY LEGS

Every day, I turned up in jeans, just like the crew and agency folks who sported their polyester flares. But the Philippines' heat and humidity were relentless. After a few days, I couldn't bear it anymore and showed up in shorts. I quickly learned this was unconventional. Crew members approached, shielding their eyes, telling me shorts were a no-go because "the boss never wears shorts" in their culture. I respected their perspective but explained my situation—feeling like I was wilting from dehydration and dripping with sweat. They seemed to accept this.

The next day, a surprise greeted me on set: everyone was in shorts, even the agency folks. They'd gone out and bought colorful satin shorts, all bright and shiny. It was a bold new look for all of us, and it brought a fun, relaxed energy to the set.

When you rented a camera in the Philippines, it came with a unique condition: you had to take an assistant from the rental house whose job was to look after it. If anything happened, the assistant would be held responsible. My assigned assistant was Fernando, a talented focus puller in his early 20s from Metro Manila—a lovely guy who became an invaluable part of the crew.

Whenever I went handheld, Fernando had to keep hold of the camera, which made things tricky, especially when we shot in a dugout canoe—but more on that later.

One day, I was lining up a shot when I felt a hand gently brushing my thigh. Startled, I looked down to see Fernando, running his hand back and forth. Confused, I asked him what he was doing. "Hairy," he replied, amused. "So much hair on you!" He then showed me his leg—easily visible with his new shorts—and explained that most Filipinos have little to no body hair. We both laughed, bridging the cultural divide over something as simple as hairy legs.

One of our commercials was for Beer Hausen, a local brew, and they were building a "German Beer House" set for the shoot. During prep, I asked Naning if we could rent a smoke machine to add some atmospheric realism to the set. In the Philippines, nothing seemed out of reach. "Sure," he replied. "I'll get one for you.

On shoot day, I arrived and started setting up the lighting. Naning loved what he saw. I turned to the props guy and asked him to get the smoke machine warmed up so we could set the level. He looked completely shocked. Naning quickly stepped in, saying he was "organizing" it and would bring it right away. As I kept prepping, I noticed a few guys bringing in sheets of corrugated iron, folded into V-shapes, but didn't think much of it until smoke began billowing from them. It looked like a forest fire—four giant smokers sending dense smoke through the entire studio. Everyone was choking, and we had to clear the set.

"What the hell are those?" I asked.

Naning explained, "You said you wanted a smoke machine. That's it!" Apparently, they'd collected dead and green leaves, doused them with gasoline, and set them ablaze in the corrugated iron "holders." I was expecting an actual machine, but this was their version. The day was slipping away, so we made do.

Four smokers were way too many, but one seemed to work reasonably well.

The eucalyptus leaves produced a blue haze that actually contrasted nicely with the warm set tones. But a new problem emerged: the burning leaves released so much ash that it was photographing—and settling everywhere: on tables, chairs, props, beer mugs, even on actors' clothes and hair. It was a mess.

We solved it by shooting in bursts. I'd light the scene, fire up "the smoker," shoot a couple of quick takes, and then we'd clear everyone to clean the set, refresh the beer (yes, it was real beer), and load fresh leaves into the "smoker."

Miraculously, we made the day, and the commercial turned out fantastic. The ash in the air added an authentic texture you just don't get from the safe, breathable alternative.

PEOPLES CRANE OF THE PHILIPPINES

Coming from Australia, Naning seemed confident I could pull off any shot he had in mind. He wanted to do crane shots in the studio and assured me they had an incredible studio crane, one that had been used by none other than Storaro and Coppola on *Apocalypse Now*.

Intrigued, I asked how long we could have it, and he replied, "As long as you want."

In fact, he'd arranged it for every day we'd be in the studio.

The first time I wanted to use it, I was setting up for a tricky shot that would require finesse, so I requested a seasoned operator. As usual, I got the standard reply: "No problem." I was excited—until I heard the gasps, applause, and saw everyone's eyes turn as the crane came wheeling in. I turned to look, and what rolled in was one of the largest pieces of equipment I had ever seen. I can't recall the exact measurements, but it must have been at least 40 feet long, with an arm three feet square. The platform wasn't just a platform—it was a full deck for the tripod, and the counterweight bucket was about ten feet long, five feet wide, and four feet deep—large enough to fit an elephant!

"Is this the crane?" I asked, a little stunned.

"Oh yes, this is the best crane in the Philippines!" I was told.

Fernando secured the tripod, and when I asked about weights, Naning grinned. "That's the best part; we'll do that once you're on."

So, I climbed aboard the platform, which they'd kindly strapped a chair to, Fernando joined me, and the Key Grip blew a whistle. Grips started lining up along the wall—more than I'd ever seen—then climbed into the bucket one by one as human counterweights. I could hardly believe it.

To steady the arm, three more grips stood on it, perfectly balanced along the fulcrum, holding hands as they maneuvered back and forth to raise and lower the crane. It was like a moving party, with people chatting, laughing, and floating up and down. The precision of these three guys on the arm was astonishing—they executed each movement flawlessly, with remarkable accuracy.

Every time we nailed a shot, the Chinese agency crew in their satin shorts erupted in applause. It was a marvel of improvisation and teamwork, and while it might not have been the high-tech setup I'd envisioned, the shots were spectacular.

SAILING TO PUERTO AZUL

Puerto Azul was a picture-perfect tropical paradise just south of Metro Manila, with a secluded, horseshoe-shaped bay, white sand, crystal-blue water, and palm trees. We were there to shoot a commercial with a Hobie Cat—a 16ft catamaran with two people on board. My first question during prep was straightforward: "The actors can sail, right?"

"Oh yeah, they're expert sailors," came the confident reply.

"Great," I said. "And we'll need a speedboat for ship-to-ship shots because Hobie Cats move fast."

"No problem, you'll have one," Naning assured me.

Fernando, who had been keeping an ear on this conversation, wasn't thrilled about putting the camera in a boat. "We don't allow that," he said. After some back-and-forth, we came to a compromise: the camera would be wrapped in a plastic bag, chained to the boat, and held in a death grip by Fernando himself. Safety first, I supposed.

On shoot day, we all arrived on the beach in our shorts—the new dress code we'd collectively adopted.

The Hobie Cat was on the water with our "expert sailors," who were already floundering, clearly having no idea how to maneuver the trampoline of a Hobie Cat. Off to a stellar start.

Then I asked Naning, "Where's the speedboat?"

"It's on its way!" he assured me.

So, we set up and waited. And waited. Forty-five minutes later, still no boat in sight. The early morning tropical light—the whole reason for our early call—was quickly fading. Then, we heard it: a faint putt-putt sound beyond the headland. Around the point came... a small dugout canoe with an outrigger and a tiny, sputtering motor. Our "speedboat" had arrived.

Fernando looked miserable.

We launched the actors in the Hobie, who immediately set off, wobbling along at about 20 knots. Meanwhile, our "speedboat" maxed out at a solid three knots, struggling to keep up. It was hopeless. The Hobie disappeared into the distance as we managed to capture a few frames: the actors falling in, the Hobie running aground, and our dugout almost being mowed down by the Hobie.

Eventually, we threw a third person—an actual sailor—onto the Hobie to keep it from veering off into the horizon.

Naning leaned over to me and asked if I could frame him out. At this point, the whole thing was a hilarious disaster. Three months later, we re-shot the Hobie scenes in Sydney Harbor, where the speedboats were *actually* speedboats.

CHASING BEER IN BAGUIO

Our next adventure was a beer commercial shoot in Baguio, a mountain town west of Metro Manila that looks like the Swiss Alps—pine trees, high-altitude views, and a winding mountain road.

Naning had planned a car chase sequence with a Porsche 944 and an Alfa Romeo, and the mountain roads were set to give it a cinematic edge.

During prep I had asked for car mounts for the shoot and of course that would be "No Problem"…I was, naturally, concerned but had faith.

I had a few other questions. "Are the stunt drivers good?" I asked, feeling cautious.

"Oh yeah, absolutely. Fantastic," he replied, assuring me all was well.

"So, real pros, right?" I pressed, hoping for a firm confirmation.

"Totally," he said, casually adding that the drivers were taking the cars up the mountains themselves.

The day came, and we left Metro Manila early. Naning, his chauffeur (who drove a Mercedes sedan at breakneck speeds) and I set off into the countryside.

It was a narrow road, barely wider than the car, weaving through rice paddies at around 90 to 100 miles per hour. Oxen, chickens, children, and people carrying anything from rice to groceries seemed to appear out of nowhere, darting across the road. As we sped along, inches from kids playing at the roadside, families eating breakfast neighbors chatting, it felt like an obstacle course straight out of a video game.

About 45 minutes into the 2 hr drive, I spotted a flash of red out of the corner of my eye. "What color are the cars?" I asked Naning, who confirmed, "Yellow Porsche, red Alfa Romeo."

"Well, I think I just saw the red Alfa off the side of the road… stuck in a building."

The driver hit the brakes, and we swung around. Sure enough, there was the Alfa Romeo, lodged right into a local hut. When I say "hut," I mean a shanty made from grass, packing pallets—anything handy. But there it was, halfway through someone's home. Miraculously, no one was injured, including the driver, who seemed unfazed. The locals helped pull the car back onto the road, where, somewhat miraculously, it still looked drivable.

Naning was off surveying the damage to the home with a huge wad of US dollars in his hand paying cash, on the spot, the way business was taken care of over there. There appeared to be quite a bit of negotiating going on, in Tagalog, but all very peaceful, lots of smiling and laughing. Apparently everyone could see the funny side of the accident. As Naning climbed back up to the road kids gathered so he sprayed them with some US dollars which lightened the mood even more.

With that we got back into the Mercedes and were quickly back at 100mph following the Alfa.

Once we reached Baguio, we got to work setting up the shoot. Naturally, I'd had a feeling there wouldn't be any car mounts waiting for us—no suction cups, no hostess trays, nothing to attach the camera to the car. Everything had to be handheld or shot as pass-bys from the side of the road. But the real kicker? The "professional stunt drivers" turned out to be, well, more demolition derby enthusiasts than precision drivers.

The first take was a letdown. The Alfa, supposedly hot on the Porsche's heels, lagged so far behind there was no sense of excitement, let alone jeopardy. Even the pass-by shots were underwhelming—the cars were miles apart, hardly the nail-biting overtaking action we needed to match the storyboards from the Chinese agency.

I decided to offer a solution. "Look, I used to drive rally cars," I told Naning. "If you're okay with it, I can handle the Alfa. We'll have Fernando operate the camera handheld from the passenger seat. I'll drive, and we'll finally get the close shots we need." Naning thought it was a fantastic idea, so I found myself behind the wheel of the Alfa, Fernando gripping the camera next to me.

We set off down the winding mountain road at about 60 miles an hour, and I kept the Alfa right up on the Porsche's bumper. During the first pass, Fernando was too terrified to roll the camera. I assured him, "Look, we're not going to crash.

I've got this—just focus on getting the shots." After a bit of coaxing (and promising the camera would survive), he calmed down enough to roll film.

Finally, we captured the close, tense shots we needed. Fernando's nerves held out, though I suspect he was more worried about the camera than himself. In the end, we wrapped the shoot with some solid footage. Despite the missing car mounts, lack of proper stunt drivers, and my impromptu rally revival, the commercial actually cut together pretty well.

THE HIGH SPEED CONVOY

After the shoot wrapped, we began the journey back to Metro Manila.

Our convoy was impressive—two "stunt cars," a van carrying the camera gear, another van with grip and electric equipment, a car for the actors, a Mercedes with Naning, myself, and his chauffeur, a couple of crew cars, and the agency people. So, about eight, nine, maybe ten vehicles in total, all cruising at a solid 100 miles per hour. It didn't seem to matter that we were on narrow mountain roads; over here, that was just the speed limit by default.

Everything was going fine until we missed a left turn at a T-intersection.

We blew past it, all ten cars in our high-speed parade, so we found ourselves pulling into a big dirt lot with a couple of shops, a police station, and a fountain in the center of a rough courtyard. The idea was to swing around the fountain and get back on track.

Now, there was a lot of political tension in the Philippines at that time. So when the police spotted ten cars barreling into their courtyard, dust and gravel flying everywhere, they didn't think "film crew." They thought "rebels." Next thing we knew, the police were scattering, diving for cover, and bolting inside the station.

We tore around the fountain like a scene out of an action movie, doing what I suppose you could call a "U-turn" (we might've slowed down, but it felt like we hadn't) and got back on the road, leaving behind a trail of bewildered onlookers and some very rattled police officers.

Back on course, about an hour out from Manila, we came upon a bridge with a crowd gathered, peering over the side. I asked Naning if he knew what was going on, and he replied casually, "Oh, probably looking for bodies."

"Excuse me?" I asked, thinking I must have heard him wrong.

He shrugged. "Yeah, the police just throw rebels off the bridges sometimes, and locals come by to… well, clean up." Apparently, that's exactly what it was: a casual community "cleanup" of sorts. We drove for a few minutes, Naning and driver chatting in Tagalog, Naning turned to me "Oh the other way around", "what", I was confused. Naning explained, very matter of fact, "The rebels throw the Police off the bridges, that's why they were all running for cover when we made the turn.

CORDON BLEU.

The first day filming was in the studio in Metro Manila. Lunch came around and and the crew were handed a bowl and a cup and stood in line for a scoop of rice and a ladle of fish head soup, with a fish head of course.

As I went to line up some people dressed as waiters appeared pushing a table on wheels. On the table was a setting for one, beautiful linen cloth and silverware fit for, well maybe the Marcos family. It looked like a meal being served at the Ritz Carlton. Naning told me this was my lunch and they set it up smack in the center of the studio….slightly embarrassing to say the least. Anyway, I was not about to indulge, I wanted to eat with the crew and not appear aloof or that I required special treatment.

After 6 weeks of fish head soup and rice I came to regret that decision.

THE CREW PARTY

Over those six weeks in the Philippines, we had some pretty funny moments, but what really stuck with me was the spirit of everyone on set—crew, actors, agency folks, director, production team, everyone was just incredible. One night, the crew was having a party at one of their homes, and I told them I wanted to go. They didn't think it was the place for me, probably figured I'd find it too rough around the edges. But I insisted—I wanted to be there with them.

Naning's driver picked up Sue and me, and on the way, I figured I should bring some beer.

I grabbed three 24-packs for about $2 each—a price that had me feeling like I'd struck gold.

We arrived to find the party in full swing: street vendors with smoky cauldrons, colorful lights strung everywhere, music blaring. The crew was thrilled, if a little embarrassed; they weren't sure their neighborhood was the "right" place for me.

Now, their neighborhood was a far cry from the typical suburb. It was a part of Metro Manila where homes were made out of General Motors packing crates, complete with "General Motors" stamped on the sides. The houses were fashioned from these crates on dirt foundations, and the floors were simply packed dirt. The street was dirt, too—barebones, to say the least.

A lot of the crew earned just a dollar a day; even the camera assistant made only five dollars daily. But despite it all, they were some of the happiest people I'd ever met. We partied until about three or four in the morning, with the Mercedes driver patiently waiting to take us back to the hotel.

That night was unforgettable. It was raw, it was real, and I was surrounded by one of the warmest, kindest groups of people I'd ever worked with. It was a far cry from what I'd expected going in, but it was a true highlight of my time there.

100 SHOTS

When people ask me, "What's the best way to become a Director of Photography?" I always say, start with documentaries. Spend two to four years, ideally four, shooting documentaries. Why? Because that's where you really learn your craft. Documentaries force you to make do with limited budgets, minimal crew, and sparse equipment. You have to navigate every imaginable situation, from unpredictable weather to unpredictable people, and find creative solutions in real-time. This hands-on experience builds up a rich mental library of techniques and tools—things you can draw from instinctively when you're working on set, especially in narrative filmmaking.

The number of times I've had to pull from my documentary experience while shooting narrative work is incredible. Those years sharpened my ability to adapt, think quickly, and create compelling visuals on the fly. When you've been in the trenches of documentary filmmaking, you develop an instinct for storytelling that can carry you through even the toughest narrative projects.

Another great way to build your skills is by working on a small series.

When I first came to America, I was fortunate to have an opportunity to work on the first season of *Tales from the Dark Side* in New York City, thanks to a chain of interconnected contacts.

I went in for the interview, and they reviewed some of my previous work. Now, I hadn't shot any narrative work at that point—my background was all in commercials, music videos, and documentaries. But they decided to give me a shot, starting with a trial on the first episode. They told me that if it went well, they'd put me on for the season.

As luck would have it, after the first two days of shooting, the producers came up to me, having seen the dailies, and said, "Okay, we've seen enough. You're on for the season." And just like that, I was in. That experience kicked off a long period of working on *Tales from the Dark Side*, which became a crucial part of my development as a DP.

The reason *Tales from the Dark Side* stands out is that it was the perfect environment to build and refine skills I hadn't yet learned shooting documentaries.

Working in episodic television, especially under tight constraints, forced me to quickly pick up new tricks—how to light for narrative storytelling, handle dialogue-heavy scenes, and frame for drama.

Every episode came with its own challenges, from limited resources to intense time crunches, but it pushed me to experiment and problem-solve in ways documentaries hadn't.

Looking back, those early days on *Tales from the Dark Side* were instrumental. It was like a crash course in narrative cinematography, but under conditions that left little room for error. I think that's the secret: find environments where you're pushed to your limits, whether that's on a documentary set or a small TV series. Those are the experiences that build resilience, sharpen creativity, and transform technical skills into an instinctive, reliable craft.

What made *Tales from the Darkside* such a unique and valuable experience were the rules and constraints the producers had set for the series.

When I first learned about these restrictions, I thought they seemed, frankly, a little silly. But as the series progressed, I began to understand their purpose. Those strict parameters were actually an ingenious way to help me build and refine a specific set of skills that would prove invaluable down the road. In many ways, the time I spent on *Tales from the Darkside* became the best "film school" I could have asked for as I moved into narrative filmmaking.

The producers had set out very specific rules: we had to shoot on 16mm negative film stock at 100 ASA, with all shots at T4. You couldn't shoot any wider than that aperture. Additionally, every single light had to be hard light—no soft lighting allowed. The entire episode lighting had to be prepped on the pre-light day, which was Friday, and we had two stages going at once with two DPs rotating on alternating schedules. One DP would prep for four days, Monday to Thursday, pre-light Friday, and then shoot Monday to Thursday, while the other DP was prepping the next episode.

The tight schedule and these restrictions meant we had to approach each episode with precision.

On Monday and Tuesday, The Director and I would sit down to develop a detailed shot list, with exactly 100 shots allowed for the episode and 20 optionals that we could use if we were ahead of schedule. Each day, if things went smoothly, we could pull five optionals to incorporate, but if we fell behind, those optional shots were immediately off the table.

By Wednesday, we'd meet with the first AD, the UPM, and one of the producers to go over our shot list, explain how the episode would cut together, and present a lighting plot showing exactly where every light would go.

This meant that by Friday, when we pre-lit the set, we knew exactly what we'd need and how long it would take—no overtime, no last-minute adjustments. Every single detail had to be locked down. If the producer objected to any part of our plan on Wednesday, The Director and I would have to adjust and re-present on Thursday, ensuring that by the time pre-light began, there was a rock-solid plan in place.

At first, working with nothing but hard light felt limiting, but it quickly became a fantastic opportunity. I'd always been a fan of film noir, and most of those classics relied on hard light.

The sharp contrasts, the deep shadows—it was a lighting style that created a sense of mystery and intensity that I loved.

The restrictions forced me to embrace those noir techniques fully, and soon I was looking forward to every episode as a chance to put those skills into practice.

Looking back, *Tales from the Darkside* provided me with an ideal environment to break into narrative work. Coming from commercials, documentaries, and music videos, I didn't yet have that honed set of skills specific to narrative storytelling.

This series gave me that experience under the tightest conditions possible.

The miles I put in on *Tales* helped prepare me for feature films and beyond, giving me the confidence and technical grounding to approach narrative work from an entirely new angle.

The lessons I took from *Tales from the Darkside* carried into every project that followed, and I can still trace so much of my foundation as a DP back to those early days on set. In the end, I couldn't have asked for a better start to my narrative filmmaking career.

TARPS, TORNADOS AND TOPEKA

We were coming to the end of an 8 week shoot on a mini series, A Matter of Justice with Martin Sheen and Patty Duke, the one Steven Spielberg liked. It was a Friday and it was Marty's last day on the show. He had to leave as he was starting on another film the following Monday so it was critical we get him shot out.

The weather had not been kind to us throughout the shoot and, as a result, we had about 9 pages of mostly exteriors to shoot and all daytime. The weather report was intermittent cloud, thunderstorms and possible tornadoes.

The main scene of the day was a Military burial at a cemetery on a hill overlooking farmlands with a small church. 21 gun salute, soldiers in uniform loads of extra's. We arrived at 6am in torrential rain and howling wind. The art department was unable to set anything up so we were already way behind schedule. Everyone stood around scratching heads, rubbing chins whilst hearing the UPM constantly mumbling doesn't matter we have to shoot.

By 8am the rain had gone, the clouds had cleared and the sun came out so we scrambled to get everything ready.

Everything was set for the first shot by about 10am, the director was panicking that we wouldn't get everything shot to tell the story, the UPM was only concerned with getting Martin on a plane that night, the electrics and grips were worried about lightning, you get the picture.

Moments from rolling on shot 1 for day the clouds started rolling in and 5 minutes later there was torrential rain. The actors all scrambled under some makeshift tents, camera's were covered in tarps, the ground was like standing in a bog. We decided to shoot close ups in the rain, covering the actors with tarps and I made the call the go for a sunny day since the weather report indicated the rain would be on and off. Tarps covered the grave, "roll camera", things were going swimmingly for everyone except the sound department. All they could hear was rain on the tarps. ADR would be necessary.

Then the rain stopped and we had brilliant sunshine again. Tarps were swung away, "bring out the extras let's shoot the wide shots". It was like this all day. The best part was during the wide shots I had sun in the foreground and a nice dark sky way off in the distance as tornadoes were passing through, about 15 miles away but brilliant sunshine and slight breeze where we were.

Late afternoon, Cemetery done, next was a crane shot for the beginning of the scene as the parents drive down a dirt road to the church and we were to finish at the church, parents exit car walk to church and our last scene was an interior.

Insurance in case we lost the light, which looked pretty definite by now. We raced down to load the camera on the Chapman Titan which had been parked in a corn field. Roll camera, action, down the road came the car, the crane boomed up combined with a subtle zoom out to a nice high wide shot of the cemetery, the hill, the church and a tornado in the distance, the light was perfect, now low in the sky, grads rolling in, polarizers...oh it was spectacular.

Fantastic shot OK lets go, we all headed to the church which was to another crane shot. Everyone was ready but the sun was tantalizingly low on the horizon. We didn't have much time and as this was the second shot in the scene it had to match the drive up and the cemetery scenes.

We all waited for the crane, the AD constantly squawking over the walkie to the drivers, lets hurry we need that crane here now. However there was a problem. The crane had sunk, up to the axles, into the cornfield, it wasn't going anywhere.

Not a big deal on the surface we could shoot without the crane BUT, it was right in the middle of the shot.

As we mulled over the situation the sun was getting lower.

Stress levels were high but I needed to remind everyone...the sun was setting.....fast. We had to modify the shot, no crane and the shot was the final part of the drive down the road, so now car pulls in, family gets out and walks toward camera...we pan around as they and other extras walk by and up to the church.

Beautiful, only problem was there was another storm brewing behind us so everything was dark and the sun was right on the horizon.

Then just as expected, pop, the sun was gone and it was getting dark fast. The director said we have to get this shot I need them arriving.

I had a plan...remember I mentioned the importance of documentaries. The sky looking to the road was lightish, the corn field was bright I suggested we set up at the steps to the small church and shoot long lens of the car down the road turning into the church parking and the actors get out and walk past camera, no pan.

By the time we would get that it would be night but I told them I could then light the front of the church for day so they would enter shot framed on the church go inside then we were inside which was no problem.

But I had to match the blazing sunlight we had for the crane shot. I had already ordered the electrics and grips to grab four 12K's and line them up from where the car would park to cover the walk in sidelight from the car past camera.

I was going to shoot wide open on the lens T1.3 and measuring the sky I knew I could get some slight overexposure, even though it was getting dark the cornfield would look good and the ambient light would be fill light, the 12K's would duplicate the sun.

I calculated based on exposure I didn't even need to rush but kept the energy high so I made sure I did not miss the point of perfect balance. No rehearsal...we have to shoot.

However, we had to wait, it was too bright and I needed it a little darker for all the elements to come into balance and make the shot work...and of course as it got dark the ambient light got bluer so we had to load full daylight blue gels into the 12K's...oh it was just like a ballet at the Met.

I told them we had time we could do a rehearsal but now everyone was panicking because it really was getting dark.

Don't worry guys, I have done this a million times, it will be beautiful.

It was pretty apparent I was the only one who believed that. Of course remember this was on film, less latitude, no monitors, no replay and nowhere near the flexibility in post that we have today....experience and photographic knowledge were the drivers on this shot. The light kept fading and finally, with the car in place I was ready. I told the director we will get two shots at this, the first will be a little bright, the second should be perfect.

It was essentially night, the director, whom I had worked with many times before asked is there any way this is going to match? "Hey no problem (I learned that in the Philippines) all under control it will be great". One last set of scrims and blues onto the 12k's and we were ready.

Martin called from the car on his walkie, should I turn the lights on...a collective NOOOO was heard echoing across the fields.

Camera rolled...nailed it. Oh, the crane, no problem, covered that with camo netting and on the long lens it was out of focus enough to give the sense of a piece of farm machinery although the script supervisor was convinced it looked like a Titan Crane. Want to do another one, sure why not. 2 takes.

Martin came to me and said "holy shit is that going to work, it looks to me like we drive down the road

on a beautiful sunny day and arrive 200 yards later at night...I guess we could say we got a flat". We laughed. Martin was a good guy and had a funny sense of humour.

We turned around swung the lights into position for the entrance to the church and there it was again, another beautiful bright sunny day...of course it was now, in reality, full night. Then onto the interior, piece of cake. As Martin said farewell after wrap he couldn't believe we made the day...a little overtime but 9 pages in the can and he would make his flight. Martin told me "you know I have a son who is a bit of a comedian...he is going to love the story about this day".

PIRATES, PARROTS AND GOLD DUBLOONS

SHHH was going to be a classic, or so I thought. I wasn't sold on the title, but it was my second feature film gig after Tales from the Darkside, and on paper, it looked like a real movie. It had a solid script, a seasoned director named Bert Cohen—an NYC commercials guy who had it all figured out—and Karen Black in the lead role. Bert was a great guy, always picking me up for location scouts in a stretch limo, which was a nice touch. He lived in a five-story brownstone on the Upper East Side and seemed to have his act together.

The concept was ahead of its time, too. This was 1984, and the story was about a magazine sketch artist whose illustrations start coming to life, revealing clues to a murder.

Today, it might be handled with an app or AI, but back then, it was a labor-intensive process. The animation would be done in Hungary, where a team of artists specialized in stop-motion sketch animation. It was complex and, to be honest, exciting. I had a solid crew from NYC and my 1st AC, a young Yugoslav named Zoran Veselic, who was the most brilliant focus puller I'd ever worked with. We started shooting, and things seemed to be moving along well—at least initially.

Then rumors started circulating. Whispers about the production's lack of funds spread through the crew, and they weren't happy. So, I had a chat with the producer and Bert, and they assured me everyone would get paid. Still, the crew grew restless. They wanted their paychecks on Fridays, at wrap, rather than waiting until Thursday after the worked week. The producer grumbled but agreed, and everyone went into the weekend happy.

Monday arrived, and so did more grumbling—this time about the catering. Crafts services were "not up to standard," as the crew saw it, and complaints went straight to the producers, who explained that we'd hit the budget limit. When Friday came around, the money didn't, and the producers promised to pay the following Monday. It seemed reasonable, but that was the wrong thing to say. The crew's murmurs grew louder, and suddenly, they were demanding to be paid day by day—an impossible demand in the film industry. I tried to keep them calm, but they weren't having it. They felt they were being conned.

To appease them, one of the producers came up with what he thought was a foolproof plan. He had a collection of gold dubloons from a Spanish galleon that had sunk off the coast of Portugal, and these were supposedly worth a small fortune. He offered to put the dubloons in the motel safe as collateral, just in case. To show his sincerity, he even gave one of the crew members the safe combination. It sounded absurd, but it seemed to settle everyone down.

The next week started, and the producers tried to pay the crew daily, but they couldn't keep up. Now the crew threatened to quit and head back to NYC. I assured the producer and Bert that my camera crew and I would stick with them, even if we had to recruit locally. The director was grateful; he'd already taken out loans against his brownstone to fund the film and couldn't afford to lose the crew.

By Wednesday of the third week, the whining reached a new level. I appealed to the crew to calm down and finish up the film. We only had 7 days left to shoot plus the Producer and Director had treated everyone very well. Great accommodation, excellent catering, 10-12hr days, it felt to me the shoot was progressing quite smoothly and I was not too worried about being paid as I knew the guys had the cash it just wasn't immediately accessible.

A meeting was scheduled for the next morning, and we all turned in for the night, hoping things would finally settle.

Around 2 a.m., I was startled awake by frantic knocking at my motel room door. I opened it to find the police, asking if I knew where certain crew members were. Apparently, there'd been a break-in. They gathered everyone in the motel cafeteria, and Bert told me the story: two crew members had broken into the office, opened the safe, and stolen the dubloons. They were on their way to Ohio to sell them. When the police asked me if I'd noticed anything, I couldn't help myself. "I saw a guy with a wooden leg, an eye patch, and a parrot on his shoulder running across the parking lot." The officer didn't find it amusing.

At dawn, the two crew members returned with cash in hand. They'd sold the dubloons to a pawn broker, getting only a fraction of their worth. The producer was heartbroken, but neither he nor Bert wanted to press charges, and since nothing else was missing, the motel let it slide. The crew members handed the cash over, but by then, the entire crew had decided to leave, except for myself and the camera team.

We spent the day discussing our options. We'd shot more than half of the film, and I felt it was worth continuing. But Bert and the producer decided to temporarily shut down, regroup, get the footage cut, and start the animation sequences. They hoped to raise the funds to finish the film. I returned to other projects, but as the months passed, SHHH quietly disappeared. Despite my efforts to stay in touch, Bert remained silent. I knew he was bitterly disappointed.

Looking back, it was heartbreaking. If the film had been completed, it could have been revolutionary for its time. But sometimes, all the experience in the world isn't enough. As I often tell young DPs, in this industry, the job is as much about business management as it is about art.

THE PITTSBURGH HEIST

We were in Pittsburgh, Pennsylvania, shooting a film called Simple Justice, starring Cesar Romero, Doris Roberts, Cady MacLean, and directed by my dear friend Debra Del Prete. One of the key scenes involved four masked men robbing a bank—We found an excellent location a disused bank that had only recently closed, conveniently located in the heart of Pittsburgh's main shopping area. It was perfect. The scene called for the men to pull up in a souped-up car, leap out with shotguns, run inside, and open fire, with one poor girl getting hit as she tries to escape. Blood everywhere, walls splattered, bullet holes and hits everywhere—it was meant to be a classic action sequence.

We set up three cameras inside the bank, capturing the action through the windows as the robbers pulled up and leapt from the car, then follow them into the back and through the scene with the final payoff being a girl getting a shotgun blast to the gut and being yanked backwards through a wall.

We rehearsed the scene, apart from the blood splatter, and everything went off without a hitch. But just as we wrapped the rehearsal, we started hearing sirens. Lots of them. The sounds seemed to come from every direction, growing louder by the second. And suddenly, six or seven police cars and SWAT vans swarmed the street, lights flashing, and officers in full body armor leapt out, guns drawn, storming toward the bank.

Apparently, someone in a neighboring building had seen the car pull up, watched four guys in masks and armed with shotguns run inside, and then heard gunfire. They'd called 911 to report a robbery in progress. Protocol demanded the SWAT team respond as though it were real, film shoot or no film shoot. So here we were, in the middle of our scene, with a dozen SWAT officers flooding the bank, guns ready, as if they were about to bust an actual heist.

Once they saw the cameras, everyone relaxed, and the tension gave way to laughter. The officers even took a moment to look through the lens and check out the set.

It turned into a pretty good time, though it was hard not to chuckle at the thought of all that high drama being sparked by our little scene. Still, it's not every day your movie shoot gets mistaken for an actual heist. We requested they do it again for the cameras…that got a good laugh but wasn't about to happen.

There's an addendum to this story. My wife, Sue, and my two boys, Ben and Paul, were there that day. Ben wanted to watch the scene so he sat beside the camera filming the girl getting hit with the shotgun blast, completely covered in plastic like the rest of us and all the camera gear—there was going to be quite a bit of blood spray. It was of course spectacular, the blood bags sprayed a couple of gallons of blood and soaked rags out over the camera, the crew and Ben and the wire pulled the stunt girl back through the breakaway wall…it was awesome.

However, six months later, it was "Career Day" at Ben's school, where each kid got to share what their parents did for work.

So, the kids went around, each proudly describing their dad's job—carpenter, fireman, doctor, lawyer. Then it was Ben's turn.

He stood up, cleared his throat, and announced, "My dad shoots ladies in banks."

About fifteen minutes later, we got a call from the headmaster asking us to come in for a little chat. "Mr. and Mrs. Draper, your son said something today that's a bit… disturbing," he said, sounding as though he was considering calling in reinforcements.

Once we explained, the headmaster seemed to understand, though I think he was still on edge. And for a moment, I wondered if he was on the verge of calling the SWAT team himself.

BOOT PRINTS IN THE DIRT

In 1984, we were in Israel, shooting an Australian TV series across Jerusalem, Masada, Caesarea, the Sea of Galilee, Eilat, and more. It was an intense shoot, with locations steeped in history and natural beauty. One of the highlights was receiving rare permission to film inside the DMZ (Demilitarized Zone) along the Jordan River—an area few crews had ever set foot in. Our fixer for the shoot was a retired General who had commanded Israeli forces in the Six-Day War. A man of few words, he guided us with calm authority and an unmatched knowledge of the terrain.

On the morning of the DMZ shoot, the General briefed us carefully. "We'll arrive at the electric fence, 100,000 volts, about one mile from the river. At exactly 10 a.m., the power will be turned off, and the gates will open. We have precisely 90 seconds to get our three cars through. Once we pass the second fence, stop, and no one gets out until I brief you again."

When we reached the fence, the General—now dressed in full combat gear rather than his usual official attire—explained that we would be under surveillance from the Jordanian side. As if on cue, the fence powered down at exactly 10 a.m., and we quickly maneuvered through the two towering fences and the rows of razor wire. Once past the second gate, we stopped, hearts racing, as a soldier approached our van.

"You will follow the car ahead, and you will stay exactly—exactly—in its tire tracks. Two soldiers will walk in front, clearing the road as we proceed." The warning was blunt but clear: the entire DMZ was laden with landmines, set to stop any enemy foolish enough to cross.

We began our cautious, painstakingly slow drive, the tension thick. As we passed a massive sand mound, we glanced back and noticed a narrow black slit facing the Jordanian side—a hidden command post keeping a close eye on our progress. Eventually, we reached the river, where we were told to stay in the cars until the area was cleared for mines. After a tense wait, we were finally given the go-ahead to set up in a small, cleared area. Jordanians on the far side of the river watched us intently from the hills, probably curious about what a film crew was doing in such a place.

As we were setting up, one of our crew pointed out something strange. The General was standing by one of the vehicles with his hands on his head, flanked by soldiers. It looked like he was being detained. Curious, we moved closer, but a soldier quickly waved us off, so we kept our distance.

Ten minutes later, the General walked back over, looking a bit bemused. He explained, "One of the soldiers spotted my boot print in the dirt and mistook it for a Jordanian soldier's." It turned out that the boot pattern was identical to the ones worn by the Jordanian Army. What the soldiers hadn't realized was that during the Six-Day War, the Israeli Army wore the exact same boots. These were the General's standard issue from his service days, but since the early '80s, the Jordanians had adopted the same boots. The Israeli army now wore boots with a different pattern. The General was impressed. As he said, he should have realized as he knew about the boot change but he was mighty impressed by the soldiers picking it up.

Even the smallest detail was not overlooked in this area.

SPRINGTIME IN MALLORCA

During the 1980s, I attended the Cannes Film Festival each year with John Hanrahan, Australia's top movie critic from the Seven Network. John and I would cover the festival for his TV show, interviewing stars, catching up on the latest movies, and soaking up the atmosphere. After Cannes, we'd usually pop up to London to shoot some behind-the-scenes footage at Pinewood or Shepperton Studios, checking out whatever Bond movie or big-budget feature was being filmed. But one particular year, EMI invited us to Mallorca instead to film on the set of Evil Under the Sun, an Agatha Christie mystery starring Peter Ustinov and a slew of legendary actors. It was too good to pass up.

So, after wrapping up in Cannes, John, my wife Sue, and I caught a flight to Mallorca. When we arrived at passport control, we confidently handed over our passports.

The officer took one look and told us we didn't have the necessary visas to enter Spain. We were

Australians and had no idea we even needed one for Spain, we did not need one for the rest of Europe.

The officers told us to step aside, and they led us to a small room that looked like a scene straight out of Midnight Express: soldiers slouched in chairs, smoke filling the air, light slanting through dusty windows, and a captain with his feet up on the table. John and I, for some reason, thought it would be fun to make light of the situation, acting out our own little Midnight Express parody. The Spanish guards, however, weren't amused.

They informed us, very seriously, that we were to be held under arrest and deported. But we couldn't just hop on the next plane. "You are under arrest for illegally entering the country," they said, promptly confiscating our passports and equipment.

We luckily had made a call to the Evil Under the Sun Production Office to let them know the situation so we figured EMI would be all over it.

However, no luck, EMI even offered to put up a $250K surety bond for us but even that was a no go. EMI did however say they would try to resolve the situation but we felt it was a lost cause at this point. They escorted us to a small room with glass walls, where we sat, watching British tourists returning from their holidays, blissfully unaware of our predicament.

Hours passed. As the day dragged on with no food or water, we started to get genuinely worried. Eventually, they allowed Sue to use the bathroom, but only under the watchful eye of a soldier with an Uzi slung over his shoulder. Sitting there, feeling the weight of our mistake, John scribbled a desperate note: "We're Australian journalists being held against our will by the Spanish police. Can someone please alert the Australian consulate or the newspapers?" We slipped the note under the door, hoping some kind-hearted British tourist would take action.

Instead, the tourists who saw it burst out laughing, probably thinking it was a practical joke. Not long after, the guards decided they would only speak to us in Spanish. Our charade had backfired spectacularly. From what we could gather, they were planning to deport us separately: Sue to Venezuela, John to France, and me to Morocco. The rules of deportation stated that we'd each be sent on the next available flight, regardless of where it was heading.

Thankfully, they scrapped that idea, and instead, we were booked on the last flight out of Mallorca—to Paris. Late that night, they marched us across the empty tarmac in the glare of tall floodlights, like hardened criminals. Four police officers with Uzi's and the police captain who had supervised us all day. We got to the plane ready to mount the stairs and the police captain turned to us and said " I hope you enjoyed your time in Spain" we told him "no we did not", he replied "good because we don't ever want to see you back here again". As we boarded, the flight captain waited at the door, receiving our passports from the guards. The crew had cleared three seats at the very back, and as we made our way down the aisle, passengers looked at us as if we'd just broken out of prison. We sat in silence, humiliated, wondering what had just happened.

Upon landing in Paris, an announcement came over the PA, asking all passengers to disembark except for "the three passengers in the last row." The captain walked back, handed us our passports, and asked what on earth had happened. We explained, and he chuckled, "The Spanish—they are so stupid."

The next day, we visited the Australian consulate,

hoping to file an official complaint against the Spanish authorities.

We were informed, however, that our chances of success were slim. The reason Australians needed a visa to enter Spain, it turned out, was due to some "unfavorable" activity: Australian mercenaries were reportedly assisting Basque separatists, and Australians were frequently caught smuggling drugs from France into Barcelona. Our reputation, as Australians, was less than stellar.

In retrospect, we were lucky. Just a few months after our trip, an Australian crew member, I think from a 60 minutes team, was shot by Spanish police in Barcelona.

Our harmless joke had nearly landed us in serious trouble, but we'd narrowly escaped with only a story to tell. And we learned one valuable lesson: Midnight Express is best kept on the screen.

As an interesting postscript I had to return to Spain several years later for another shoot. I arrived in Barcelona and as I approached passport control I was a little nervous. I don't think I have ever been so polite to a customs official. He looked at my passport, went to pass it back, then pulled it back and looked again, carefully turning the pages…oh oh I thought, this can't be good. He opened a page then looked at me I smiled, he smiled, he reached for his stamp, thumped it down, handed the passport over and called next.

SELF PRESERVATION

GAFFER FROM THE CRYPT

After months of persistence, I finally got my break on *Tales from the Crypt*. I'd seen the first season on HBO and was immediately hooked; the series looked incredible. Executive producers Dick Donner, Bob Zemeckis, Walter Hill, and David Giler had developed something fresh, dark, and visually arresting. As soon as I discovered that Bill Teitler, whom I'd known from *Tales from the Darkside*, was producing it, I hit the phones. After nine months of calling, I finally landed a gig: flying out from New York to shoot the wraparounds with the Cryptkeeper.

Dick Donner wanted a fresh look for these scenes, shifting away from the multi-colored comic book style of season one. I started working with Kevin Yagher, the SP MUFX wizard and the mind behind the Cryptkeeper itself. On the first day, the Execs loved what they saw, and just like that, we were off to the races.

During the shoot, Kevin shared that he was up to direct an episode and mentioned the script. Set in a 1920s sideshow, the episode called for an entire carnival set to be built on a soundstage. After reading it, I knew I wanted to shoot it, so I went straight to Dick Donner. He was on board as long as Kevin approved, and soon I was locked in. It was my chance to shine, and I went all in. Twelve months later, that work paid off when I took home the show's first CableACE Award for the episode, *Lower Berth*.

By that time, I'd shot several episodes, working with a lineup that included Michael J. Fox, Teri Garr, David Hemmings, Mariel Hemingway, and Rita Wilson. It was a who's who of Hollywood. Bill Teitler had moved on by my seventh episode, and a new producer had stepped in, bringing along his own sidekick. As luck would have it, they'd scheduled a particularly tough episode with an intricate scene set for Friday night. While I was out scouting locations, my gaffer relayed that the producer wanted an early wrap and requested I find a way to shoot the scene without using condors to raise the lights.

I looked it over, talked it through with the director, and confirmed we could make it work. I had the gaffer inform the producer that we were good to go. We wrapped the scout and arrived back at the studio in the early evening. I was making my way to my office when one of the PAs told me to stop by the producer's office. I walked in with a friendly greeting, only to be blindsided. I was fired on the spot, told to pack my gear, and "get the fuck out." It was no joke. There was no explanation, just the door. And with that, my time on *Tales from the Crypt* came to an abrupt, thunderous end. I had shot some of their best episodes, delivered their first CableACE Award, and yet there I was, with absolutely no idea what went wrong.

Eighteen months later, I was prepping a miniseries with Robert Wagner and Donna Mills in Palm Springs, a production for Len Hill. The series was produced by Ron Gilbert, one of the toughest but fairest UPMs I'd ever worked with. We'd been scouting locations and were back at the hotel when Ron called me to the production office late that evening. He had something urgent to tell me.

When I arrived, Ron got straight to the point. "I know why you got fired from *Tales from the Crypt*," he said. He explained that my former gaffer from *Crypt*, now working with us on the miniseries, had been in his office all evening, spinning tales of what I supposedly would and wouldn't do on set.

It turned out that this same gaffer had stirred up trouble back on *Crypt*.

Fortunately by this time I had shot several movies with Ron. He knew me well and was completely thrown by what the gaffer was telling him as it was totally out of character.

I was astounded and discovered after I had told him to let the Producers know I would work out a different way of shooting the night scene so they could make their early wrap he told them "Draper said absolutely not, I have one way to light it and that's what I will do I will not have my lighting dictated by a Producer"....no wonder they canned me on the spot but it would have been nice to have had an explanation. Ron picked up his phone and called the gaffer in his room "I need to speak with you now", by now it was about 9.30pm. Ron told me to head back to my room and he would give him the same treatment I got on Crypt.

The moral of the story: Never stop covering your back which is why between 1991 and 2000 I worked with the same crew on more than 50 projects.

PITCHING

Canada is a fantastic place to work, and Vancouver has always been one of my favorite cities. Between shoots, I'd often zip up to Squamish and Whistler to hit some of the best mountain bike trails around. This particular job, however, didn't leave much time for outdoor escapades. I was shooting a TV movie, well into the final week, when my assistant camera (AC) casually announced that he was leaving to work on a feature film and introduced me to his replacement. Shocked? Absolutely.

I pulled him aside, suggesting it might have been considerate to let me know beforehand rather than showing up with a new guy like a done deal. If he'd had the decency to tell me in advance, I wouldn't have had an issue. But he clearly thought he was irreplaceable, despite having a bit of an attitude. After a brief, heated exchange, he generously offered to finish out the day before disappearing into the ether.

Now, this was the '90s, and I'd shipped up two of my own ARRI 535 packages from LA. The AC, however, fancied himself a "Panavision man" and made it clear he didn't care for the ARRI. As we wrapped for the day, I went to the camera truck to say goodbye, only to find he'd already left.

Around 4 a.m. the next morning, the dailies supervisor called from the lab. There was a serious problem with the footage from the A camera. I rushed to the lab, and sure enough, the image was bouncing all over the place, completely unusable, it would definitely need a reshoot…which was the first, and only, reshoot for technical reasons in my career. As soon as I saw it, I knew what had happened.

The ARRI 535 has a pitch control knob to adjust the sync between the pull-down claw and the registration pins in the gate, where the film momentarily stops for exposure. The control had a range of positive and negative adjustment to essentially control the sync and thereby manage the noise level of the film passing through the camera. It required careful but simple setting. During the previous day's shoot, I'd noticed the camera was louder than usual and had asked the AC multiple times to check the pitch control. Each time, he assured me it was fine, claiming the 535 was just "a noisy camera."

Fact is, it wasn't. I'd owned those two ARRI 535s for nine years, shooting more than 40 projects with them, and I knew how quiet they could be.

When properly set, the 535 was one of the quietest 35mm cameras around. But here's the kicker: the pitch control had been cranked all the way, either positive or negative, throwing the entire camera's sync off. The result? A loud, shaky mess, with footage that was totally unusable.

Of course, there were denials, but it was clear what had happened. Despite how good the movie looked overall, the damage to the dailies meant I never worked with that director or producer again. Meanwhile, the AC was off on another job, likely convincing someone else how indispensable he was.

The lesson? Work with people you know and trust. And if you don't know them well, or suspect a problem, check it yourself.

A BRIDGE TOO FAR

I have always been terrified of heights, one time whilst filming in Paris, my son Paul and I decided to take the elevator to the top of the Eiffel Tower and walk down the steps. Both of us could barely get our legs to operate but, put a camera to my eye and I will hang out of a helicopter, stand precipitously close to a cliff or teeter on a bridge.

Way back in about 1976 I was tasked with filming the opening of a new structure, The Sheahan Bridge. The new concrete and steel structure was replacing the historic *Prince Alfred Bridge* over the Murrumbidgee River at Gundagai, New South Wales. The old bridge was completed in **1867** and stood as the longest timber viaduct in Australia at 921 meters (3022 feet). Serving as part of the Hume Highway for over a century, it connected Sydney and Melbourne and was a significant engineering feat for its time. This made the Prince Alfred Bridge around **109 years old** when it was retired from service. Traversing it was an experience, it rattled and shook and clanged and vibrated as everything from a bicycle to a 16 wheeler traversed its planks.

So, back to 1976 and the opening. There was to be a parade, the local cops, fire engines, ambulances, farmers in their tractors, school kids, bands all for the grand opening by the Premier of New South Wales, Neville Wran. There was a crowd, I was shooting for the nightly news and needed some good overall shots. I climbed up on a railing behind some of the crowd, threw my trusty CP16 on my shoulder and filmed away. Jumped down, reeled off some other coverage and headed back to the station. The following morning on front page of the local newspaper was a shot of the Premier cutting the ribbon and me, standing on the 4" wide railing filming, not realizing there was a drop of about 100 feet if I made the slightest miscalculation. It was a great shot and to this day I still have flashbacks and tremors thinking about where I was.

WINTER IN NEWARK

THE STREET

The Street was a gritty American police drama that aired in 1988, with a unique production style that set it apart. Created by John Mankiewicz and Daniel Pyne, at the time writing for Miami Vice. The series followed the lives of two pairs of patrol officers working the night shifts in Newark, New Jersey, capturing their encounters with crime and the complex social dynamics of their beat.

The series took a cinéma vérité approach, shooting largely at night with handheld cameras, lending a realistic, documentary-like quality to its visuals.

Each episode ran for 30 minutes, totaling 65 episodes that aired five nights a week in syndication. The use of frank language and mature themes meant it often aired after 11 p.m. in many markets.

The show featured notable actors like Stanley Tucci and Michael Beach, and it garnered attention for its intense, raw portrayal of police work, setting a standard for later procedural dramas focused on street-level perspectives

The Street was indeed a groundbreaking show, driven by a unique challenge from Sid Sheinberg, then-President of Universal Studios. Sheinberg put out a call for someone willing to produce a police drama series on an extremely low budget of $100,000 per episode—far below industry standards, especially in comparison to *Miami Vice*, which was then produced for around $1 million per episode.

Most in the industry turned down the challenge due to the intense budget constraints and fast-paced schedule, but Bob Pittman, who had made a name for himself by launching MTV, accepted it.

The show's concept was raw and gritty, focused on street-level police work, with the intention of capturing a real, documentary-like quality. John Mankiewicz and Daniel Pyne served as executive producers and writers, bringing in young producers Bob Altman and Steve Bawol to drive the project.

The demands were nearly unprecedented: they needed to shoot and complete one full episode per day, aiming to wrap each episode by the end of the day's shooting—a grueling pace that felt almost "biblical," requiring 40 episodes in 40 days.

We mulled through how this was going to be shot and it was decided documentary style, hand held, single camera. Other elements were that the show would be covered, literally in three shots.

Essentially the camera would become a participant in the scene. A further element was absolutely no cutting so there would be no masters and coverage, each scene would play out in a single long take.

From my perspective, as we developed the style of the show, I became more excited as it really became a fantastic exercise for a cinematographer. The scenes would have to be lit fast since most of the locations had very little available light. The entire show was to shoot at night on the streets of Newark and there was to be no cutting of the camera and no coverage.

The scripts were written with the three shots described as OLI (outside looking in), ILO (Inside looking out), Hand Held (everything outside the police car). This in itself threw up some crazy challenges.

The original idea was to shoot 35mm but for me that was totally impractical. The camera's were too big and heavy and the amount of gear we would have to carry would simply slow us down. I suggested at first going to 16mm but that also was impractical. Shooting an episode each night on film meant we would not see dailies for two days so by the end of the week we would have 5 episodes in the can but would only have seen the dailies for two, maybe three. If we were shooting an episode a night and there was no going back, shooting on film simply was not practical.

The only solution, as I saw it, was to shoot on video. Something that had never been done in the US for a network TV series.

I was not too concerned as before moving to the US I had been thrust into the ENG world, literally overnight, when my CP16 was switched for one of the first ENG style video camera's, the RCA TK76 and I did not mind shooting on the format as I simply applied my film techniques to the parameters I was given in the camera….and it all worked well. Plus I liked the immediacy.

The advantages of video were numerous. The camera's were light, especially ENG style camera's, there was access to good zoom lenses so no lens changes and we could play back each take to make sure we had the scene. As I was also operating it gave me the freedom to shoot true documentary style and move the camera through the scene getting establishers, overs, close ups, reverses, etc all within the one shot by creating a dance between the characters and the camera. It didn't take a lot of convincing that this was the approach we should adopt so my next challenge was, the camera.

I was familiar with most of the video camera's available at the time. All analog of course. SONY had launched the Betacam which had taken over in news gathering and I heard they were about to launch a new version of the Betacam with better low light sensitivity, better colorimetry, a little bit more compact. I got hold of the new camera through SONY and shot some tests. This was definitely the way to go.

The first five scripts arrived from Daniel and John and we set to work prepping. Before we started shooting we had the luxury of about one week to prep the five episodes.

Locations were chosen so there were no company moves and essentially we would shoot around a city block. Photographs of the locations were sent to Daniel and John and they would write the episodes to the locations.

After the first week of shooting we would no longer have the luxury of prep. Five scripts would arrive on Saturday morning by Fedex overnight, I would have Saturday and Sunday to prep, I would arrive early Monday afternoon with the crew for a very quick scout and the instant night fell the camera rolled.

The first night shooting was a little chaotic as everyone learned the ropes of what was essentially a totally new way of shooting a tv series. But by the end of the first night we had some great feedback on the technique and some good ideas for improvements moving forward.

The actors loved the style. For them it was like a stage play, they simply played the scene. We would spend 2-3hrs blocking the scene and working out the choreography. When we shot the scene the rule was three takes and move on so it was three shots to shoot the show, no cutting and only three takes. Almost absolutely true documentary style…and it worked.

We wanted to be more ambitious than just seeing the police car drive up or doing long scenes in the car so we devised a plan to get the camera in and out of the car so we could shoot a scene in one location, cops and camera would get into the car, we would literally drive around the block continuing the scene then at the next location actors would already be into the next scene, cops and cameras would get out and join them and continue on…all without cutting.

To facilitate this the police car was wired with lighting and microphones. When we shot a scene the sound recordist was safety'd to the roof of the police car and would boom the scene from the roof, as the cops transitioned to the interior he would cross to the internal mikes and at the next location back to the boom.

Keep in mind this was January and February…Steve was not at all thrilled when the scripts called for these shots….which became a regular feature.

To make the cop car interiors more interesting I had the key grips build a speed rail dolly for the back. We took out the rear seat and bolted speed rail to the floor. Then took a rectangular piece of plywood and screwed skateboard wheels to it so we had a sliding dolly for the back seat…affectionately dubbed "the asshole dolly". As I approached the car an assistant would take the camera holding a predetermined frame, I would quickly jump in the back onto the dolly and the camera would get passed in to me then off we'd go. Sometimes I would get into the car ahead of the actors with the camera passed through the window so I could slide across the back as the actors jumped in and the appearance was the camera was dollying from outside to inside the car. The dolly also gave me the ability the get better angles sliding back and forth between actors for essentially French overs and also allowed me to lean well forward into the front seat.

After the first five episodes we pretty much had the show nailed down. It was a hoot, shooting an episode per night doco style was both creative and fun.

A new Director would come on each week but essentially there was not much for the director to do as the writing and the choreography essentially dictated how the show would be shot…some just sat back and enjoyed the experience.

SONY took some interest in the show and wanted to see the first week's dailies as they were keen to know what the camera could do as it had not been released. When they saw what we were doing they took the side plates, with SONY emblazoned on them, off the camera, they weren't too sure this was how they wanted their camera to be viewed. However, a few weeks into the shoot some preliminary screenings for advance PR were held. The reviews were sensational, so SONY reps returned and put new plates back on the camera with their shiny name clearly visible for all future behind the scenes shots.

The show was an awesome experience. Reviews were sensational "Practically creates a new visual language" said the New York Times, "TV will never be the same again" LA Times…some of the reviews were full page the show was so revolutionary. The sad part…no-one saw it. The show was buried in late night 11pm on syndicated tv. It never ran prime time Network. Essentially it was an experiment, that worked.

Following The Street I had several calls for new cop shows that wanted to have the same style. When I explained how we created it they were not enthused, still being rooted in 35mm standard techniques. I was never hired for the shows and they attempted to create the same style shooting the way it had always been done but it just didn't work.

My favorite was some shows attempted the cinema verité look by having the camera on a gear head panning back and forth and tilting up and down very slightly throughout a scene. It just looked ridiculous, but most were simply too scared to go all out and shoot the shows using our style.

I used to joke in interviews that the style we created for the Street would basically destroy television and would give way to eventually be the accepted way of shooting…of course now we have "reality" television but that is covered my multiple camera's. Noone has been brave enough to shoot an entire show hand held, single camera, three shots per episode, an episode per night, on location, since.

WISH YOU WERE HERE

SELFIES IN PARIS
(Casablanca, Barcelona, Budapest, NYC & Somewhere in Greece)

Wish You Were Here was a 1990 American sitcom that aired on CBS as a summer replacement show. It starred Lew Schneider as Donny Cogswell, a Wall Street stockbroker who, after a particularly rough day, quits his job and embarks on a European backpacking adventure, sending video postcards home to his family and friends. The show was quirky and relied on the camcorder craze of the time, capturing Donny's travels and interactions in various cities. It sadly only ran for six episodes

In the summer of 1990, I got a call to shoot *Wish You Were Here*, a new summer replacement series for CBS, with my pals from The Street, producers Bob Altman and Steve Bawol at the helm. They had come up with another doco style series idea. The concept was unique: we'd follow Donny Cogswell, played by comedian Lew Schneider, as he explored Europe, "sending" video postcards back to his friends in the U.S. Each episode would feature Donny's travel adventures, with him talking directly to the camera, as if he were sharing his journey with friends—a precursor to today's selfie-driven travel vlogs only "waaay" ahead of it's time.

We initially thought about shooting on 16mm film, but quickly realized it wasn't feasible. Being overseas, we wouldn't have time to wait for film to be processed, view dailies etc., so video was our only choice. I did some research and discovered Sony was about to release a professional Hi8 video camera. Compact, lightweight, and capable of high-quality footage with interchangeable lenses (which meant I could take short and long focal length zooms), the Hi8 was a perfect fit. Plus, it allowed us to work inconspicuously, which was a huge advantage since we'd be filming around landmarks in Paris, Barcelona, and Morocco, without permits.

We wanted to look like a small documentary crew, keeping a low profile with just Lew, myself on camera, a sound guy and director. Meanwhile, away from the action would be the producer and script supervisor on headphones listening to what was going on. Once the director had a take he likes we would play it back and if everyone was happy, move on.

The real trick was figuring out how to make it look like Donny himself was holding the camera while walking through famous sites. We wanted a casual, immersive style, like he was having a personal conversation with viewers and had to be talking directly into the lens. I decided I would operate the camera while walking backward with the camera on my shoulder, with

Lew holding onto my wrist, just below the lens, which helped keep him framed and focused as I moved. We practiced by doing each shot in reverse to get the timing so we could transition smoothly from a moving shot to a static tripod shot without any cuts. When Lew reached the static point, he'd grab the matte box, and I'd guide the camera into the tripod's lock so that he could run back in the shot, take up his predetermined position in the frame and continue talking, with it appearing as though he'd placed the camera there himself.

One moment that still makes me laugh happened on the Champs-Élysées in Paris. A woman overheard us speaking and asked, "I heard you guys are American, what are you filming?". "A TV series for CBS," I told her. She just looked at me, smirked, and said, "Right," clearly thinking it was some kind of prank or DIY project, and continued on her way.

"Wish You Were Here" was another revolutionary endeavor for its time. It was years ahead of what we now know as selfies but that is essentially what we were creating…if only we had realized at the time.

BABY ON THE BOSPHORUS

In 1985 I was asked to shoot a documentary series by my old pal Martin Johnson. The two of us started together at RVN2 in Wagga, and years later I was living in New York City. I'd only just moved over there, and Martin called me to do a second series, the first series we'd shot in Israel, and there's a brief mention of that in Bootprints in the Dirt, an earlier chapter in this book. He wanted to go and shoot a 24-part documentary series on the life of the Apostle Paul all through Europe and the Middle East.

The only problem was we had to go and do a location scout for a couple of months, and then when the 3-month shoot was scheduled, Sue and I were due to have our first son, so it created a bit of a dilemma, largely financial. The move to the US had cost us a fortune and work was sporadic as I was starting fresh in a new country, not to mention the toughest market, and we needed the money so I had to do the film.

As it was an Australian production, we decided we would fly back to Australia. Sue would have the baby in Sydney, and I would be off in Europe and the Middle East shooting the documentary series, and as it turned out, I didn't get to see our son until he was three months old.

There was a silver lining and that was Sue had her family and friends around which would not have happened had we been in the US for the birth….so I kept reiterating what a positive that was, sometimes I think on deaf ears.

We had scouted just about every Roman city between Rome and Israel so there was a lot of travel. We rented a 50-seater Mercedes-Benz bus out of Munich in Germany that we converted with 747 Business class seats up front, tables and benches as a production area in back and of course, a great galley down below. We had been assured the Greek driver, George, was a brilliant driver and cook.

Zoran Veselic was assisting again. We spent 4 days prepping the camera gear at Arriflex in Munich, loaded up the bus and then we headed to Rome to meet with the rest of the Australian crew, who were flying in a few days later.

We left Munich very early morning the day after loading the bus because George wanted to be well down the Autobahn before there was any traffic. We crossed into Austria early in the morning and George suggested stopping for breakfast at a huge rest stop above Innsbruck. We pulled in and as we did another tour bus pulled up beside us. On the destination board of the bus was "American Millionaires".

Zoran, George and I were grabbing jackets as the passengers on the other bus were offloading. Big belt buckles, cowboy boots and 10-gallon hats. Our door hissed open and the three of us stepped out. The millionaires looked on and George closed the door. One of the millionaires asked, "aren't the others getting off"?

I told them "there are no others, just the three of us, where are you guys off to" "Oh we are on a tour all 50 of us, for 10 days around Germany and Austria, how about you" Then I couldn't resist spinning a yarn "Well Zoran and I do this every year, we get George and we just travel around Europe for 6 months"

"God damn" was the reply "yeah we don't like

travelling with lots of people so we bought this bus and keep it stored in Munich then call George up, fly in and off we go".

Needless to say they were impressed.

By now most of the millionaires were in the restaurant, the three of us came in ordered, ate up and got up to leave. As we stood to exit all the millionaires waved to their obviously wealthy new friends….we waved back. They all came to the restaurant window to watch us climb into our Mercedes Tour bus and drive off, south to Rome.

But that was not the story I wanted to tell….

We scouted something like 300 locations, Roman cities, every one of them on top of a hill and the idea of the documentary was to shoot the entire series in the perfect light, either magic hour morning, magic hour afternoon, or unusual weather conditions (eg rain, snow, very overcast, etc), but never to shoot in the middle of the day in bright sunshine. I didn't want the series to look like a travel show. That plan didn't always work for us but over the 3-month shoot but we managed to stay pretty true to the plan.

So, we headed off on the shoot. All over Rome

then down to Brindisi. Across by ferry to Greece, 2 weeks in Greece then on to Turkey.

After several days in Istanbul we headed south as we had the obligatory day of shooting at Gallipoli which is on the Dardanelle Strait connecting the Aegean Sea with the Sea of Marmara. Gallipoli was the site of what was essentially an ANZAC bloodbath at the hands of the Ottomans during WWI.

We spent a dreary morning, overcast and raining, filming in Gallipoli, and I was anxious for our late lunch break at Canakkale on the eastern shore of the Dardanelle.

So we finished our shoot at Gallipoli and crossed the Dardanelle by car ferry to Canakkale. We weren't going to be in Canakkale long as we had a 400km drive east to Selcuk for the following morning shoot at Selcuk Castle followed by a couple of days at the Roman ruins in Ephesus.

We found a small restaurant, and when we went into the restaurant, George (the bus driver), who was Greek but also spoke Turkish (and several other languages), talked to the owner and said, look, we've got to make a phone call to Australia because this guy here, his wife's having a baby, and we need to get on to them so he can see what is happening.

It was only a small restaurant, but everyone in the restaurant new my wife was in Australia having a baby, and then the word went out around the town like wildfire. Soon townspeople, entire families, kids, store owners came in and gathered around, and in the end there were about 150 people inside the restaurant and outside leaning through the doors and windows waiting to hear what was happening on this phone call.

The problem in Turkey was when you wanted to make an international phone call, you had to book the call about seven hours in advance. So the owner dialed to talk to the operator who explained, well, we can book it, but it'll be in seven hours. The owner yelled into the phone, in Turkish, "no, absolutely not, it has to be now because it's a man here, an Australian man, and his wife's having a baby in Australia".

The funny thing was everyone in the town kept apologizing to us for the massacre of Australian soldiers in the First World War at Gallipoli. We kept saying to them, look, it was a long time ago, don't worry about it, we're not here to punish you for World War I, but everyone kept apologizing regardless, so they wanted to go out of their way to make me feel happy. After several minutes of the store owner yelling at the operator and a chorus of yelling from the those who had gathered. The operator said she could not put the call through.

Now it was time for George, ever the diplomat, to take the phone. He got on and started speaking to the operator in a very quiet calm tone, and then there was a lot of yelling, and the store owner was yelling, and all the people inside and outside the restaurant were yelling, everything in Turkish, and the owner was yelling louder, and eventually the operator agreed to put the call through to the cheers and applause of the crowd.

Then it was my turn. The store owner heard the phone ringing in Australia quickly called me over and suddenly you could hear a pin drop. Total quiet. "Hello Royal North Shore Hospital", I told the person on the other end who I was, where I was and that I needed to speak with my wife. "Sure let me put you through to the ward". I told George, he translated for the crowd, they all cheered, then total quiet again.

"Hello this is the maternity ward", I quickly explained the situation and the response "I'm sorry she can't take a call we don't have a phone near her bed", "Well can you take one to her", "no we can't do that", "well, can she come to the phone?" "I don't think so, she is in a bed connected to a monitor and drip" "I don't care what she is in, wheel her bloody bed out to the phone, I am in Turkey and have been waiting for 7 hours to place this call…get her to the phone". There was a lot of mumbling in my audience and a lot of shuffling on the other end of the phone….eventually I heard Sue's voice on the other end of the phone. I signaled thumbs up to my audience, they let out a communal cheer. We talked for about 5 minutes, all th locals listening intently and not understanding a word. Labor had just started so I would be on the road with no communication for the next few hours….I figured by the time we got to speak again I would be a father.

An addendum to the story: After our unforgettable stop in Çanakkale, we set off for Izmir, not knowing what was waiting for us up ahead. The moment we left town, the skies opened up, unleashing a torrential downpour. Thick, dark clouds swirled above us, and the sky was alive with flashes of lightning and the rumble of thunder echoing across the hills. It felt as though the storm had a life of its own, growing wilder as we climbed up into the low mountains, winding our way through the mist and rain-soaked roads.

Just as we reached the top of the climb and leveled out onto a plateau, the storm seemed to hold its breath. The rain stopped abruptly, and the clouds parted just enough to let shafts of golden, late-afternoon sunlight pierce through like a series of celestial spotlights. The landscape before us transformed into something surreal, almost otherworldly. Beams of sunlight danced across the plateau, casting a kaleidoscope of colors and shadows across the wet earth, while the dark clouds hung low around us like theater curtains framing the scene. Out to our right, the ocean shimmered under the fractured light, alive with hues of deep blue and fiery orange.

Our stills photographer, who was on the shoot to capture images for a book on the series, was seated up front looking out at the spectacle unfolding to the south. Turning back to me, he called out over the hum of the engine and the hush of the moment, "Mark the time—your son has just been born." I looked down at my watch, realizing this wasn't just a routine timestamp. It was a moment I'd remember forever. I noted it down, and as it turned out, I was off by only two minutes.

The drama of nature felt like it was marking the occasion with a show of its own, as if the heavens had opened up to celebrate. In that brief, powerful display of light and shadow, it felt like the universe was somehow acknowledging the arrival of my son—halfway around the world.

COULD YOU PASS THE ROMANÉE CONTI?

The film *Sex, Love, and Cold Hard Cash* wasn't exactly the title anyone had in mind, but that's what it ended up being called. It also seemed the title did not really warrant the consumption of Romanée Conti, but that's Hollywood.

The Movie was directed by my old friend Harry Longstreet, with his wife Renee, the producer. Part of the story was set on a cruise ship, so naturally, our prep demanded a trip to look over the cruise ship and what better way to survey the ship, in exactly the right light, than a four-day cruise from Long Beach to Ensenada, Mexico, to scope out potential locations on board.

Harry, Renee, the first AD, and I boarded on a Friday night, ostensibly to work, but Harry was a bit of a wine buff. Every night, we found ourselves in one of the dining rooms sampling multiple bottles of Opus One, whilst the script, written by Harry and Renee, called for a romantic scene where the characters order a bottle of Romanée Conti, a wine that goes for around $4,000 a bottle. We were getting in the mood.

Over dinner, Harry mentioned he'd draft a letter to the vineyard in France, suggesting they send us two bottles for free in exchange for the "publicity" the film would give them, an idea we all agreed was absolutely brilliant, especially given we only needed one bottle for the scene, the other Harry, Renee and I could….sample.

Our four-day cruise was exhausting. Breakfast on the poop deck followed by scouting the area around our table…perfect we all agreed. Then a couple of hours to rest up and a scout of the aft deck. "Perfect but we will have to come back to check it out for the night scene, maybe after the cabaret". Then it was time for a massage followed by drinks or a meal. We did check out various spots—staterooms, restaurants, night locations—it was tiring but the Opus One each night for dinner made it worth the effort.

When we got back, Harry sent the letter off to the Domaine in France. A couple of weeks later, he received a curt reply from the vineyard: they didn't need the publicity. If he wanted the bottles, they were available for purchase—at full price, of course. Determined not to be deterred Harry decided to buy two bottles anyway BUT he was not going to waste it on actors.

The bottles arrived and the day of the shoot Harry called in the props guy to his stateroom to carefully open and decant the wine, then had him refill the bottles with grape juice, meticulously resealing them so they looked untouched.

That day during filming, Harry kept the original wine in his stateroom, and for a couple of nights, after wrap, we'd head to the room to savor the real Romanée Conti. Meanwhile, on set, the actors were blissfully sipping grape juice out of the "genuine" Romane Conti bottles. At one point, an actor commented on the "fruity" taste, prompting us to explain that, unfortunately, all we'd been able to get was the empty bottles, which we'd filled with grape juice. We never let on that the real wine was being thoroughly enjoyed in Harry's stateroom each night.

SHORT ENDS

CAN I HAVE YOUR AUTOGRAPH

I was driving my Ferrari up I95 heading home to Maine after the car had been in Boston for a service. Just over the New Hampshire Maine border I pulled in to a rest stop. Before I could get out of the car there was a guy tapping on my window. I rolled it down. "Hey how's it going?" I said politely. The conversation that followed was a little bizarre. Now I was wearing a cap and sunglasses.

The Guy: "Oh man I have to tell you I absolutely love your movies"

Me: "Huh"

The Guy: "Yeah Close Encounters was the most awesome movie and really when I saw that I just became addicted to movies"

Me: "Well that's fantastic but I am not Steven Spielberg"

The Guy: "Oh yeah I know, I know, you have to say that just for privacy but oh man all your movies are just amazing"

Me: "Look, that's great but I am not Steven Spielberg"

The Guy: "Oh OK…..then who are you?"

Me: "Look I am just a guy driving home and I have to go to the bathroom"

The Guy" "Oh OK OK…sorry man"

Me: "No problem"

I got out of the car (locked it just in case) and went to the bathroom. When I came out the guy was still there.

The Guy: "Hey I know who you are, you're James Cameron" I laughed..

Me: "No I am not James Cameron"

The Guy: "dammit I know you are somebody, Are you sure you're not Steven Spielberg?

Me: (chuckling) "Yeah I'm pretty sure"

As I got into the car the guy pulls a piece of paper

out of his pocket with a pen

The Guy: "Well can I have your autograph anyway?"

Me: "Sure…what's your name"

The Guy: "Martin"

Me: "OK Martin I'll tell you what I'll do. I will give you my autograph but you have to promise me you won't look at it until I am driving away…deal?"

The Guy (very excited) "Oh yeah absolutely that's awesome thank you."

I took the paper and pen and jotted down a note folded it and made him promise again not to read it until I was driving away. I handed the note over, started the engine, backed out and slowly drove towards the Interstate entrance, watching in the rear view mirror. Martin opened the note, slapped his hands on his head, spun around, waved to me, looked back at the note.

The Note : Martin, it was wonderful meeting you today and thank you for all the very kind words. Best Wishes. Steven

BILLIARDS AND GOLF BALLS

During Tiger Warsaw, we were working 6-day weeks so Sunday was out free day. Looking to get out of the hotel Patrick Swayze, Bobby DiCicco, my assistant Zoran and I decided we would go play golf. None of us were golfers. To spice the game up a little we rented a golf cart and took along a cooler with some ice and bottles of whisky, vodka, tequila and gin…I think we may have had a few beers. The idea was whoever lost each hole had to do a shot.

Now taking a cooler with alcohol on the golf course was actually not allowed so we needed to sneak that in under the guise of being water and sodas. Also, the course was totally booked. There were no tee times available all day, so we requested special dispensation. We were told to arrive early and ask golfers ready to go if they would mind if we jumped in front. The first group we asked agreed. It was a decision they would soon regret.

We teed off on the first hole a 367yd par 4. My ball went about 50 yards, Zoran's went the farthest, about 80 yards but off in the rough to the right, Patrick was in a lake to the left and Bobby hit a tree and the ball rocketed back towards us with us all ducking for cover.

We finally got far enough down the fairway that the group behind could start or so we thought. Golf balls were whistling by us, it looked like they knew how to hit them.

We got to the first green and all had scores in double digits. We pulled the golf cart aside and decided we had better all have a drink, it was going to be a long game. We allowed the group behind to play through.

By the time we got to the third hole we had allowed two more groups to play through and it was pretty obvious this would not be an 18 hole game. The stocks of alcohol were already getting low.

We continued on, holding up players coming from behind, moving aside at each tee to let one or two groups play through. I think we finally made the 9th green. Zoran was lying on the ground using his putter like a billiard cue when we got a call to come off the green. An official said the club had apparently been getting complaints from golfers that we were holding them up and may have been intoxicated and that is would probably be best if we returned the golf cart and left. To be honest we were ready to call it a day anyway. We had downed a little more alcohol than we intended, we were sunburned and I think we all had scores well over one hundred and had pretty much had it with golf for the day.

We apologized to the official. He asked for Patrick's autograph, returned the cart and called for one of the PA's to come to the golf course to drive us back to the hotel.

We did not play golf again but the following weekend Patrick and I decided to go line dancing on a Saturday night.

TEQUILA IN OHIO

Patrick was just coming off his popular TV series North and South and was becoming a household name. His popularity meant it was difficult for him to get any privacy so he largely stayed in the condo the production had rented and we would go over for drinks or just to sit around and shoot the breeze. One time we were treated to him, with guitar, giving us a rendition of his new song "She's Like The Wind".

We were wrapping early on a Saturday and Patrick asked if I would be interested in finding a country bar somewhere out of town for a bit of a peaceful night and a few drinks. We were shooting in Sharon PA and just across the State Line was Youngstown OH so we figured we would head west and see what we could find.

It didn't take long and we found a country and western bar that wasn't too crowded so we decided to give it a try.

When we walked in we were obviously the new kids in town, the place didn't stop but close to it, while everyone watched us walk up to the bar. As we took a seat the dancing started again and all seemed fine.

Patrick loved Tequila, I was not too sure and following that night I had decided….I hated Tequila.

After a couple of rounds of Tequila and a couple of beers, I think all they had was Bud, we were approached by one of the local guys…."so man, why are you coming in here trying to look like that dude Patrick Swayze, the TV guy." Patrick quietly replied "I don't know sorry but I didn't come in trying to look like someone or to do anything other than have a drink with my friend". The guy seemed to relax a little but added "Yeah well my girlfriend thinks you are Patrick Swayze". Patrick smiled the Swayze smile and said quietly "Just tell your girlfriend I am not Patrick Swayze and sorry I look like him, I am just a guy having a drink"

That seemed to appease the guy, he sauntered off but was quickly back with his buddy and their girlfriends. Almost in unison the girls piped up "You really do look like Patrick Swayze but I guess you're not him why would Patrick Swayze ever be in this joint? Everyone laughed, well the four of them, we might have smiled. I piped in "we thought this place was kinda cool"…they didn't want to hear from me.

Now one of the young ladies chimed in, "If you were Patrick Swayze, and I'm not sayin' you are, but if you were why would you be here?"

Patrick, again with the classic easy-going smile replied, "probably because I just wanted to get a drink and have a nice quiet evening with my friend"

With that they seemed satisfied that we were just two dudes getting a drink at a bar although they did keep giving the squinty eyed glance but now the girls were getting bored…one of them said "Oh OK, (to the others) let's leave them alone I want to dance some more."

The guys liked the sound of that…and with that they left us with "have a good one" to which we replied "thanks"…waited a moment, quickly paid our bill and left. It was a situation I had seen quite a few times, the ability to have celebrity and anonymity was simply an impossible dream.

The funny thing was the barman turned to Patrick as we were leaving "Look I won't say anything but you actually are Patrick Swayze, right, you're shooting that movie in Sharon?" Patrick nodded the affirmative, shook the barmans hand and we were gone like the wind.

THE STORM BUILDS

It was a single line in the script, "Remember Me" based on the novel by Mary Higgins Clark and starring Kelly McGillis and Cotter Smith.

We were shooting at an old lakeside mansion on the northern shore of Lake Ontario east of Toronto.

The house was huge, 4 stories and we had built a widows walk on top for the climactic scene. But **the storm builds** was the start of of the run up to the climax. The Director and Producer wanted it to be spectacular so we went all out.

The night we arrived to shoot the scene, and remember this scene was three words, the area looked like a full on construction site. I had a lighting unit built on a 150' construction crane called the Dwight Light. It was 144,000 watts of light made up of 144 1000 watt lamps in four banks of 36 that could all be independently rotated and focused. I needed something tall as the lights needed to be at least 120' in the air to light the area and to allow for the full wide shot of the house. The light was powered by a separate 28 foot generator truck. There was a second 150' construction crane with two "spinners" to deliver the rain and two 24 foot water trucks to provide all the aerial water we would need. I had two 60 foot condors with rain for the sides of frame and four 20 foot rain towers behind camera. Each side of the house had a ritter fan. The ritter is essentially an airplane propeller in a cage, they produce an enormous amount of wind. The interior of the house was lit for the mood of the upcoming scene and we decided as it was a quick shot in the script we would only shoot with one camera although the Director and I got nervous and figured we would shoot two cameras for safety, we were shooting film.

We had a 4 hour earlier call to get set up and rehearse and the rigging electrics and SFX guys had been there almost all day.

The Producer was Sonny Grosso. Sonny was the NYC cop who was the actual guy who broke The French Connection. He had been a consultant on the movie and decided he liked it so much he would leave the police force and become a movie Producer.

As the Director, Michael and I arrived, Michael said to the driver…don't stop keep driving. It did look like the whole thing was out of control. We pulled in and there, in a trench coat waiting for us was Sonny….he wiggled his finger at us….that "come over here and lets talk kind of wiggle. We wandered over and Sonny put an arm around each of us "boys this is costing me a lot of money…it had better look good"

We both assured Sonny it was going to look amazing.

As night started to fall it was time to do a rehearsal with all the elements. The Dwight light was so bright it could have lit all of Yankee Stadium so I only had one bank on at about half power…I justified it by acknowledging I needed the height.

The scene looked fantastic, the rain, the lighting was going to work beautifully when it was dark, the wind, the debris being thrown in by the greens folk…all we had to do was wait until dark.

I wanted to shoot with the last glimmer of light in the sky so the trees behind and to the side of the house would be silhouetted faintly against that last glimmer of blue in the sky but still looking like night.

We fired everything up, it looked amazing, the camera rolled 10, 15, 30 seconds, cut. That was it, all that effort for 30 seconds. We decided to do it one more time 1. Because it looked so good and 2.

Because it seemed all that effort was worth more film. The second take was brilliant as well. Everyone was happy and now it was time to move inside and shoot some real scenes.

Each morning I would get a call from the lab to give me a dailies report and I would get a call from the dailies supervisor who was overseeing the transfer of each days dailies to video. The dailies colorist called me about 6am. Which was unusual, I rarely heard from him. "Hey Rob, I had to call and congratulate you that shot you did last night was one of the best miniatures I have ever seen". Shocked I replied, "what do you mean we didn't shoot any miniatures last night", we had shot miniatures a few days earlier of a train crash at a level crossing, I figured he was talking about those shots. "Oh, the train, yeah thanks that stuff looked awesome". He said, "no, not the train the house, that shot looked amazing how big was the miniature". I explained it wasn't a miniature it was a real house. "Oh really, I could have sworn it was a miniature, oh well it looked great anyway".

I was anxious to see dailies when they arrived on ¾" UMatic cassette, remember those? Sure enough, he was right, the shot looked great and did what was intended but because we had shot it so wide we lost the scale, much the same as trying to shoot a mountain so it looked like a beautifully executed shot of a dollhouse. However, audiences did not notice that and for them it was simply "The Storm Builds"…just as the script intended.

TORCH THE CABIN

In the mid-to-late '80s, I worked with producer Jeff Abelson and director Doug Dowdle on a few music videos, with the first being Bonnie Tyler's *Holding Out for a Hero*. Jeff and Doug were pioneers in the development of music videos as promotional vehicles for feature films, a trend that took off in the '80s and early '90s, and they were responsible for many of the big ones during that era.

The shoot for *Holding Out for a Hero* was elaborate, blending western themes with dramatic visuals. We filmed on the Veluzat Ranch in the Santa Monica Mountains which was famous for its authentic western look and feel and was used in a large number of westerns. The shoot was complete with dancers, cowboys, and horse chases—all shot to look like scenes from classic westerns like *Hopalong Cassidy* or *The Rifleman*. This meant a lot of "day for night" shooting, which involved carefully manipulating the daylight to look like night.

The horses posed an interesting challenge that none of us were aware of until the day of the shoot. Due to regulations, the horses could only run across the frame once and then had to rest for half an hour. So, we'd load the cameras onto a camera car do one take with the horses, then unload and move on to shoot dancers or other parts of the scene while the animals rested, before going back for another horse pass. It was like juggling multiple productions in one.

The climax of the video was an intense scene with a log cabin that was supposed to catch fire as Bonnie Tyler rushed out. The whole day had been quite windy, and the fire marshal kept going back and forth on whether it was safe to proceed with the cabin burn. The entire set was in suspense, waiting for the final word. By then, it was late, and the set was buzzing with over 200 people—dancers, choreographers, camera crew, grips, electrics, hair, wardrobe, makeup, animal wranglers, cowboys, actors, and Bonnie's entourage. Jeff, the producer, was getting anxious about going into overtime with so many people on set and his anxiety was bubbling ever closer to the surface.

Doug and I were on the crane trying to work out the timing of the crane move and a combined zoom when finally, the fire marshal gave us the go-ahead and said right you can do it but you only have 15 minutes. Jeff, feeling the pressure, suddenly shouted out, "Torch the building!" Doug and I were still on the crane, trying to rehearse the shot, and we yelled back, "We're not ready!" But Jeff wasn't hearing it. He barked, "I don't care, roll the fucking camera—the building's getting torched!" Before we knew it, the cabin was ablaze. Bonnie wasn't even inside yet, but with no choice, she darted into the now-burning cabin for the shot. Dancers ran into the shot dancing. "Cowboys…where are the fucking cowboys" screamed Jeff…they came running in. We were holding waiting for the flames to get a little higher and everyone to be in position, someone shouted "do the shot Bonnie is getting barbecued in there" I think Jeff called action and we were off.

With the flames climbing and the set crackling around us, we rolled the camera and swung the crane in for one take. There was no going back—the cabin was already consumed in flames. The expression you see in the final shot of Bonnie Tyler running out of the burning cabin is completely genuine—pure adrenaline, surprise, and the raw urgency of that single take. The song finished and by now the cabin was well and truly ablaze. We were still rolling and asked Bonnie to jump in front of the camera so we could get some shots of her and the cabin burning but the fire Marshall had already called for the hoses. There were firemen hoses, backlit spray, steam everywhere…I yelled down to Jeff this looks fantastic….his response at the top of his voice "I don't give a shit did we get the shot?"…..The shot was fantastic.,

That was the dramatic, fiery climax of *Holding Out for a Hero*. It was a perfect example of the unpredictable madness and magic—of music video production in the '80s.

FORGETTING THE CRAZY

During the documentary series I shot across Europe and the Middle East, I captured some of the most breathtaking aerial footage of my career. Back then, we didn't have the luxury of gyro mounts or stabilization gear designed for filming; or at least that could be rented cheaply for documentaries, it was all raw and handheld. I'd sit on the edge of an open helicopter door, usually a Bell Jetranger with one door removed, secured only by a safety harness attached to the floor, with nothing but my camera in hand and the open air around me.

The helicopter shots in Turkey were especially unforgettable. We filmed in ancient sites like Ephesus, Cappadocia, and Pamukkale, each place revealing incredible views from above. When we moved on to Israel, I filmed over Masada and Caesarea, where we had military pilots eager to show off their skills. These Israeli pilots were incredible—they could practically read my mind. The closer they could get us to the water, cliffs, or ancient structures, the better they seemed to like it.

They would execute every maneuver I suggested, and if I asked for a tighter pass along a cliff or a quick descent over the water, they delivered with a smile. Everything was shot magic hour with the light making everything even more spectacular. Shots over Masada at sunset were incredible.

But the real daredevil was a Turkish military pilot we worked with at Pamukkale. This guy wasn't about to be outdone. When I told him how skillful the Israeli pilots had been, he grinned and took it as a challenge. Flying low over Pamukkale's iconic limestone terraces, he hovered so close that people below were ducking for cover. At one point, we skimmed over the edge of the cliffs, and the helicopter's skids actually touched the limestone—an experience that felt as much like a heart-pounding thrill ride as it did a shoot.

In Ephesus, we filmed along the ancient roadway that once connected the harbor to the amphitheater. Our presenter was down on the stage in the amphitheater connected to audo via radio mike, and as we flew low and close for the shot, I heard a peculiar pinging noise. I had a headset on so I asked the pilot what the noise was, and with a calm I'll never forget, he said, "Don't worry. It's just the police shooting at us because we don't have a permit." The bullets didn't deter him in the slightest; we completed the shot, swooping around the amphitheater, capturing breathtaking footage, and flying on, as if dodging bullets was just part of a regular day's work. Which I guess for him it was.

One of the most spectacular moments of the entire series, however, was our time in Rome. I filmed from a helicopter travelling the length of the Via Appia, the ancient Appian Way, leading into the heart of the city. Early in the morning, the streets were still quiet, as we flew along the old road, at sunrise. Though the Colosseum was never directly at the end of the Appian Way, we couldn't miss the opportunity to film an aerial of it at sunrise so there I was, hanging out of the chopper curving up and around the Colosseum itself, just as the sun illuminated its historic arches. That sunrise over Rome, the ancient stones bathed in golden light, was one of the most awe-inspiring sights I've ever captured.

These helicopter shots were an exercise in trust, but the pilots were amazing and highly skilled and that skill allowed me to capture some of the most memorable, unforgettable shots of my career.

.

ABOUT THE AUTHOR

Rob Draper, ACS is an internationally acclaimed Director of Photography with just on 50 years in the industry. Known for his innovative approach and willingness to push boundaries, Rob has been a pioneer in high-definition and digital cinematography following on from 30+ years in film.. His extensive body of work spans major Hollywood studios, television networks, and independent filmmakers worldwide.

Starting his career shooting TV news in rural Australia, Rob quickly advanced through documentaries, commercials, and into television, eventually working with industry giants like Universal, Paramount, MGM, and Warner Bros.

His cinematography on *The Spitfire Grill* won the Audience Award at Sundance and set a record for the highest sale price for an indie film at the festival.

Rob's pioneering visual style helped redefine TV, earning him the first Cable ACE Award for Cinematography on *Tales from the Crypt* and critical acclaim for his revolutionary work on *The Street*, praised by The New York Times as "practically creating a new visual language" His commercial collaborations with companies like Arriflex, Fuji, Sony, and Panasonic have made him a valued consultant in developing film and digital technology.

In 2004, Rob shot Australia's first entirely HD feature film and soon launched Visionmill, his own HD production company, which created the world's first HD-originated internet TV channel, Singlemalt TV.

Currently, Rob continues to contribute to the industry with recent work on Four seasons of *Creepshow*, as backup and 2nd unit DP on 3 seasons of *The Fosters* and multiple feature films. In addition to his on-set work, he has been a mentor to thousands of cinematographers around the world.

A HAIR IN THE GATE

www.ingramcontent.com/pod-product-compliance
Lightning Source LLC
Chambersburg PA
CBHW070549170426
43201CB00012B/1776